A LITTLE BOOK ON FASTING

Luccas Laq

I am deeply grateful for the assistance and encouragement provided by my friends Athena, Alison, Ryan and Harry during the writing of this book.

At last, but equally important, I am grateful to you, for purchasing this book and being part of the health revolution.

GREETINGS

I present myself not as some master living on top of a mountain, but rather as a friend who is a few steps, or at most, a few miles, away from where you're currently at - not necessarily ahead, not necessarily behind. This book is meant as a signpost along the way; a map; or, better yet, as a trail that I leave behind as I continue my way towards the peak that I envision - and whatever lies beyond it.

What's written here is not meant to be taken as professional advice. It reflects my personal experience and perspective only, and not the universal truth. Therefore the only thing I recommend is being sincere with yourself and following your own intuition and inspiration, breath-to-breath. In other words, this book is not going to tell you what to do or directly change your life, because only you have the power to do so. However, I do have plenty of advice on what *not* to do... so to those who are willing, this may be used to facilitate your own journey.

You somehow found your way here, so I

sincerely wish you find value in the following pages. Just keep in mind that both challenges encountered along the way and magnificent transformations you may experience will be your own doing.

"Your soul is drawn to the things that will help you unfold your most glorious expression. Give in."

- *Cynthia Occelli*

CONTENTS

1. WHAT IS

To fast means to cover one's mouth. Essentially, it means to abstain from the consumption of any particular form of energy or substance, which could range anywhere from excluding particular food groups, solid food altogether, water, anything perceived as a drug or stimulant, or even avoid gazing at liquid crystal displays and using the internet, withdrawing from social activities, or a vow of silence for any determinate length of time.

It is an opportunity to turn our attention within, and to analyze and explore the depths of ourselves. This way we may be able to become familiar with and inhabit every inch of our bodies, leaving no stone unturned, no trauma unaddressed, no organ impaired and no impurities sabotaging our lives.

Over the decades, we added our own problems and addictions to our lives by doing things. To fast is to enter a state of not-doing - at least temporarily, which in turn allows healing, or undoing, to take place. To heal, or to be healthy, is to become whole again; by purifying, regenerating and re-integrating every aspect of our being.

However, it is not a mysterious or complicated practice at all. What's mysterious is the buried parts of ourselves, the suppressed emotions, and the idea of leaving our comfort zones and overcoming addictive behaviors. To let go of emotional crutches and face who we really are. In other words, it is to do consciously what already happens unconsciously every night: to withdraw from the outside world and venture into the dark, the realm of our subconscious. All of us are already fasting for 4-10 hours every night. Choosing to expand this time frame willingly allows the innate intelligence of our body to do its work to a greater extent.

"We cannot solve our problems with the same thinking we used when we created them."
- *Albert Einstein*

Most problems arise from improper or overconsumption. Therefore it would only be foolish to think of solving it with more consumption... The answer is in the elimination of what's already inside. Nothing we put in our body heals the body; only the body heals itself. At best, certain substances can assist the process, while most are only a hindrance.

It is most important to understand that we are not starving, "losing" weight or harming ourselves when we fast. We are "winning", or rather re-claiming, our health. Most of us already find ourselves in a chronic state of being "dis-eased", as our bodies have all sorts of accumulated waste and toxins. When we stop overloading the body with dense foods on a daily basis, it simply reallo-cates energy freed from digestion to something it is already doing most of the time: detoxification and regeneration. So once we hit a certain hour mark, the body understands that food is not going to come in, and shifts into "cleaning mode" - usu-ally somewhere around 48 and 72 hours, which is also when one may stop experiencing "hunger pains".

We do not feel tired or uncomfortable be-cause we stopped eating food. We feel tired be-cause the body takes this opportunity to do a big house clean, which it may have never had the chance to do in *decades*. Therefore most of our en-ergy and resources are redirected to the elimin-ation of waste and the repair of organs and tissues. We may not be seeing it in real time, but the body is doing a tremendous work-in.

Most of the "weight" is being shed, not lost, because it is actual dead weight. Our body encapsulates toxins with mucus to isolate them from healthy cells, which most people call "fat", or water retention. Most of us are puffy and swol-len because of this, and since this is a chronic and global issue, we have lost the reference of what a truly healthy body looks like. So that extra "weight" goes away as the body has a chance to purge the stored toxins. "Thin" is simply a contrast in reference to the common standard - but why would anyone want to carry around extra, useless baggage anyway?! Let go of what doesn't serve you, especially if it's holding you back.

Everyone has easily 5-10 pounds of dried waste in their intestines, even if they are already lean (speaking from experience), and who knows how much people with large bellies actually have! Getting to a week into fasting will allow a complete new perspective to be realized (spoiler: the majority of people would still be pooping).

At last, after eliminating most of the foreign material, the body has another task, or rather, an opportunity: it can get rid of its old, damaged cells and create new, healthy and optimal ones to substitute them. It will *never* destroy healthy cells, especially those that form our vital organs. Most of us have started building ourselves in an unstable, rotten foundation - which gets worse with each passing generation. So it is not enough to simply clean everything... afterwards, to achieve true, long lasting health, it is necessary to tear down the faulty construction and rebuild a new, solid, optimal foundation. Only then our bodies will start to achieve their true potential, and a temporary state of being "underweight" is left behind to embody a natural state of health.

This can't even be compared to the swollen state from before, and it is a process that happens gradually and in relation to the state we found ourselves in when starting to shift, how fast we change our lifestyles, and how far we are willing to go. There are no limits except the ones we perceive for ourselves.

Therefore, the "low energy" phase is temporary, and it also comes in cycles of detoxification; whenever we dig into a deeper layer of tissue. It is a constant cycle of purging, reaping the benefits of achieving a healthier state of being, and then back to purging... It is recommended to sleep as much as you can during a fast, and to only exercise and move around to the degree you have the energy to, and is comfortable with - and that will vary on a day to day, week to week basis. Respect yourself. There is a time for being active, and a time for being passive - it is all about finding the proper balance for *you*, where *you* currently stand.

Our body is the only temple that really matters - it hosts our awareness, soul, or I AM presence. Whether we are at peace and healthy - at ease, or in pieces, fragmented - dis-eased, affects our whole perspective and experience of life, as well as which types of energies and entities will inhabit our temple. Choose your company wisely!

2. WHY

"Everyone thinks of changing the world, but no one thinks of changing themselves."
-    *Leo Tolstoy*

Do you dare to be the exception? Changing oneself is a prerequisite for anyone who truly wants to change the world - it must start from within. There is no better gift to offer the rest of humanity than our own self-transformation and the unfolding of our highest, truest potential.

There's a common lesson, in the form of a story, about how a frog would die in a pot of water if you slowly increase the temperature, but immediately jump out of it if you put the frog inside it when it's already boiling.

We're not so different... The human potential for adaptation may be the most remarkable feature of our bodies. For better or for worse, we get used to things, but that doesn't mean we're immune to them, or that a sacrifice isn't made to put up with it. Our body is always doing its best to keep us alive, regardless of what we do to ourselves. It can be difficult to spot patterns of sabotage when they've been ingrained in us from an early age, and reinforced through the course of not only years, but decades. Especially when most of our peers are engaging in similar behavior - we've come to a point where it's normal to be unhealthy, to the degree we've even lost sight of what being healthy actually feels and looks like. Most people are miserable and suffering in one way or another, but the majority of them decide to either hide it or suppress it with drugs; sometimes legal, sometimes illegal. All in an attempt to meet others' standards and expectations...

To anyone who thinks their food choices are optimal, or even acceptable... Why not fast on water or juices for 3 to 7 days, and then consume those again and see how the body responds? Most of us feel uncomfortable upon simply skipping a meal, which is a great indicator of how unhealthy, dependent and damaged we are. Humans can survive several weeks without "food" and several days without water, but only a few minutes without breathing.

The worst you feel during the beginning of a fast, the worst is your current state. Anyone who can jump into a 3 days water fast without notice and casually go on with their lives without issues or discomfort is in great shape. Why not put it to test yourself? You know, just to be sure you're not unconsciously limiting your life span because your body got used to potentially unhealthy food preferences... At the very least you'll acquire a neutral perspective and an opportunity to re-evaluate your habits from it, as opposed to simply following trends or secondhand information (such as this very book). Nothing beats what we learn and confirm through our own experience.

Another good story I'd like to present is Plato's cave allegory. In it, people have been chained inside a cave since birth, in such a way that they can only look at the cave's wall. From behind them, there is a fire, and a group of people that uses tools to make all sorts of different shadows in the wall, which is all the information the chained people are aware of. One day, some-one frees themselves by accident, and wanders outside the cave. At first the person is very con-fused, and the light from the outside world hurts their eyes. Gradually they get adjusted to it, and begin to rejoice in the wonders of their new real-ity. However, they decide it would be unfair for them to enjoy these pleasures on their own, and go back to the cave to tell and attempt to free the others.

Back in the cave, the person struggles to reach the prisoners, as their eyes are no longer adapted to the dark environment of the cave. Then, with great excitement, they begin to de-scribe the wonders of the outside world, how the shadows in the wall are but an illusion created by a group of people who manipulate them, and how they could also free themselves from their chains and venture outside. Communication is difficult. Not only do the chained people deem this person a lunatic talking nonsense, once a few of them attempt to peek behind their backs, looking at the fire hurts their eyes, which makes them both angry and scared.

From here there are two possible outcomes. In the first, the prisoners kill the person who came back in an attempt to save them, which reflects how they're not ready to question their perspective of the world and would rather dismiss even the idea of leaving their comfort zones. As the character Morpheus said, it must be understood that most of these people are not ready to be unplugged. And many of them are so inert, so hopelessly dependent on the system, that they will fight to protect it. You can't forcefully wake up someone from a coma, and much less those who are only pretending to be asleep.

But there are those who are only half asleep, on the verge of waking up... In their case, a gentle whisper in their ears is all that is needed. So in this other outcome, a group of prisoners dare to test if what the stranger said is true, free themselves from the chains with their help, and venture outside the cave, where they confirm with their own eyes what words could only have hinted at.

It is essentially the Matrix storyline, and there are many other myths and stories that draw from similar principles, such as the Hero's Journey as described by Joseph Campbell. Not much has to be said about the people who make shadows with the fire and fool (manipulate) the people who are chained... they are not necessarily specific individuals, but rather, certain institutions and customary beliefs that are sustained through the centuries, only superficially changed in order to adapt to the current times of each generation. For instance, it's not like slavery was ever truly abolished... it simply changed form into something that can be accepted as "humane" by today's standards.

We can also look at the chains as our addictions, because in truth no one chains us but ourselves, or unless we, consciously or unconsciously, give our consent. The darkness of the cave is both the comfort zone and a reflection of the state of ignorance (limited perception) people are living in. It can be said that looking at the fire is short term fasting and the beginning of the cleanse, as it can be very uncomfortable at first, but then one gradually adapts and starts to realize they actually have been in a cave, and there's something beyond it. The older someone is, the longer they've lived in darkness, the more the light is likely to hurt their eyes... because the more damage and toxins have accumulated over the decades. Then, going outside the cave would be long term fasting, through which one can fully transcend (trance-end) their current experience.

In reality, there are many caves... or perhaps one cave, with many levels. It can be said the rabbit hole might actually be endless. Who would know? The deeper we look into the mystery of life, the deeper it is... All of us have been more or less living inside of a box in some way or another, until we are presented with new information, either through other people or our own experience, that in turn makes us question our current beliefs.

Then we have the choice of staying where we are or going beyond our perceived limitations. One of these caves relates to our food choices. No matter what one thinks about food, the only natural thing for a human being is to drink their mother's milk during infancy. After that, we *learn* habits and customs from our family and society, and carry on with these without knowing whether or not they are, in fact, to our best interest. To have been doing something for several generations is in no way a good reason to keep doing it, otherwise we would never see any form of progress. To evolve means to outgrow our current boundaries, to develop something new, or to find new, more efficient or satisfying ways of doing something. It is an expansion of horizons and possibilities, and therefore, a shift of realities.

A major problem with food is that we've

been conditioned to eating certain things for decades. In fact, for generations. And now we've even gone beyond the realm of different types of whole foods, because some things are grown with pesticides and artificial fertilizers, others are genetically manipulated, and many others are heavily processed, altered, and mixed with chemicals made to enhance their flavour, increase durability, and so on. How could any of these be considered natural? The biggest issue, however, is how disconnected we became from the whole process. One can't even begin to compare something grown in their own backyard, with love and care, to anything store-bought, regardless of whether or not it has a certified organic label.

In the past, it would have been much easier to do a water fast and get things more or less straight. Nowadays, there are so many references, and so many addictions, and so much confusion, that the situation seems rather complicated. The solution, however, remains simple, even if it doesn't seem so at first glance.

When we shift to seeing the whole picture, the universe is always in harmony. Only when we isolate aspects, moments or parts of it, there can be an illusion of chaos. Opposites both depend on and define each other. And there's always a continuous flow of light and darkness, summer and winter, day and night, construction and destruction... So if on one side we have been ingesting artificial substances that cause harm to our bodies, in one way or another there's always a solution for it at hand. For example, decades ago we wouldn't have fast access to as much information as we do today. While water fasting may have been the optimal cleanse in the past, now we have juicing machines, and a great availability of herbs and other tools that can assist the process. Any teenager can invest a few dozen hours on the internet and become considerably knowledgeable in a subject, or at least get enough information to where they can begin to apply it.

It is also worth discussing what is natural. I consider natural anything that is spontaneous and self-sustaining. The cycles of the sun, the moon and the stars are natural. So are the seasons, and likewise many species of plants and animals continually sustain themselves. Most machines, GMO foods, hybrid crops that depend on fertilizers and human assistance, plastic and many others are what I would consider synthetic or artificial, because they depend on humans for their propagation. Of course we are part of nature itself, so my definition is debatable. But if we went extinct, so would these.

Anything that is natural, or self-sustaining, has an innate form of intelligence that is akin to the very essence of the universe, or what some people may refer to as [God]. Our very cells are in touch with that essence, given how they are always doing their best to keep us alive, regardless of our choices and circumstances. All of our organs and glands function by themselves, without our conscious interference. To visit doctors or take drugs that alter the functioning of our bodies is to dare say we somehow understood this intelligence, or became superior to it, which is far from the truth. Even science admits that it doesn't know the function of most of our DNA, and that our human brains only work at a fraction of its full potential. What *is* our full potential, anyway?

"There are no chemical solutions for lifestyle related problems."
- *John Rose*

People love to relinquish responsibility for their problems, to blame external circumstances, bad genes, or bad luck, or any other excuse they can come up with. Those are the same people that are too afraid to unchain themselves and explore the unknown; to see for themselves whether or not they have been living in a cave of ignorance. The truth is no permanent change will ever happen unless we first make permanent changes in ourselves, and our own lifestyles and mental attitude. Whether we think our health is outside of our control, or whether we own it as a result of our daily habits, will determine our fate. That is, we create our own fates through our personal choices. The vast array of possibilities is always there, just like entering in a buffet and observing the infinite choices available. What will you choose?

Ultimately, it is crucial to decide for yourself why you are doing this. What exactly you are trying to achieve, heal, or transform - so you can remind yourself of this in the challenging moments to reassure you it is worth continuing - and I can guarantee you, *it is*. But just like a hike to the summit of a mountain, you won't be able to see the full view until you take the last steps. All you get are small confirmations along the way, such as the purer air, and the unique perspective of looking back and around from your new vantage point.

Both a vision of getting in touch with the divine, or even transcending our needs and becoming a God or a Goddess ourselves, looking a few years younger, or simply wanting to reduce the number shown on the scale are equally valid reasons to fast - so long as they come from a place of love, and not self-punishment.

One must fast because they want to, and not because they think they have to, or heard that they should. It is a path that must be experienced willingly and chosen responsibly in order to yield the most, and long-lasting, benefits. It's not something one should guilt-trip themselves into or do because it became trendy. If you don't learn to appreciate the process, with all its ups and downs, and know *why* you're going through them, you won't be satisfied with where it will lead you afterwards. You must find the right reasons for *you*.

Especially because it is not always a walk in the park. It is more akin to a training, or some sort of self-initiation. When a sedentary person begins to workout, it won't be fun at all. Most people have a hard time when they begin to learn any skill or discipline. And most long duration projects are daunting in general, regardless of whether they are related to business or to our own bodies and minds, which is what leads most people to quit not too long after starting them.

With fasting, or improving our food choices and health in any way, it is no different. That's why I highlight the importance of developing a *strong personal reason* for engaging in it, and understanding an overall of what the process may be for the average person, by searching other's stories and transformations. That's mostly what will keep you going, until you begin to reap the rewards - which are inevitable for those who persevere long enough.

3. STARTING POINT

"Vitality and beauty are gifts of nature for those who live according to its laws."
-     *Leonardo da Vinci*

There is a great deal of confusion in regards to what is optimal for human consumption, but I won't address or compare diets in this book. After all, we are talking about living, not dying. I am more interested in lifestyles than death styles. Fasting will improve your health regardless of what you decide to eat, and as a result, a natural refinement of your preferences towards what is truly optimal for you will be inevitable.

However, despite the neutral stance assumed, it must at least be recognized that most of what fills the shelves of supermarkets and people's fridges is not even food to begin with. There are worlds of difference between anything that is a whole substance and something that comes in a plastic container, with a long list of artificial, isolated ingredients. Forests create life, food and medicine, while human laboratories and factories are only able to make drugs.

From my perspective, there is only one disease, and its name is constipation. If we're not eliminating properly, we are accumulating something... and it doesn't take an engineering degree to visualize how any obstructions in circuits, or inside systems that rely on circulation, can be hazardous. The more resistance there is, the more energy will be required to maintain its functioning, and the more impaired or limited its potential will be. Are we eating in order to sustain or to limit ourselves?

As per Einstein's $e = mc^2$, we know that everything in the universe is waves of energy vibrating in different patterns: an orchestration of electromagnetic frequencies. It could be said energy is light matter, akin to the yang or positive principle, while matter is simply dense energy, akin to the yin or negative principle. The same essence, with different qualities being expressed. Without a perception of contrast, there wouldn't be experience.

Therefore life, or health, can be seen as a rhythmic, optimal flow of energy. The state of being unhealthy, or dis-eased, or in suffering, is to have obstructed flow, where friction creates havoc and energetic dissipation. If life is music, obstructions are noise. Death is simply no flow, or complete stagnation and stiffness - it isn't called rigor mortis for no reason.

The breath is what animates our physical bodies. Spirit is latin for breath, and holy comes from whole. That's a possible interpretation of what the bible means by the state of being inhabited by the holy spirit: to be able to take whole, deep breaths. While we're at it, I find it worth mentioning that the etymology of inspiration means divine guidance. Therefore you're not filled by the holy spirit or able to receive proper inspiration if your diaphragm is not using its full range of motion, that is, if one is taking shallow rather than deep breaths.

Our breathing is the most important vital sign, and the very measurement of life itself: it is both the first and the last action of any conscious being. To breathe is to be alive, and how we breathe determines how we live.

Borrowing Arnold Ehret 's formula as a base: V = P - O. That is, vitality equals power minus obstructions. Vitality, or life, is equal to power, or the flow of breath - prana or energy if you prefer, minus the obstructions and physical blockages clogging the insides of our body, which in turn not only limit the functioning of the diaphragm, but also suffocate ourselves on a cellular level. We don't die because we "grow old", we die when, for whatever reason, the human body becomes so constipated and rigid that the breath of life can no longer flow through us. That's why, in his book, Ehret came to the conclusion that our bodies are essentially air-pumping machines. Anyone who has a qualm with these ideas, or the very notion of "breatharianism", is invited to hold their breath and see what happens first: thirst, hunger, or passing out due to hypoxia. At least to me, the pyramid of our needs is very clear.

Whatever limits our breath is limiting our life.

Whenever one consumes inflammatory foods, a mucus response is triggered in the body in order to isolate that substance. We could say that whatever was ingested disrupted the internal balance of the body (homeostasis, or peace), creating a state of imbalance (conflict, or war). Normally the body would eliminate these things through the back door, or the skin, coughs and sneezes, while some people claim it also happens through our kidneys, and at last, things such as vomiting or diarrhea happen in the more extreme cases of intoxication. A problem arises when too many inflammatory foods and too many toxins are ingested on a daily basis, more often than the body is able to eliminate them, which in turn results in their accumulation.

It is worth pointing out that stress also

causes inflammation, and foods are not the only way toxins get into our body, as the city air and water supply are also very compromised. Most things that are alive have a negative charge, while most things that are dead, or dying, have a positive charge. That's one of the reasons why the air on top of the mountains, in the middle of forests or near the ocean is so healing: it is charged with negative ions. Living things in nature, such as trees and plants, produce these. On the other side, electronics in general, and most of the electrosmog in the cities, are known for generating an abundance of positive ions, which are detrimental to our health. The same can be applied to whole, natural, organic, ripe, and ideally raw, foods, as opposed to anything that's been isolated, enhanced, genetically modified, refined, microwaved, or denaturalized in any way.

A parallel can also be made with the pH scale, where from 0-7 we have acidity (positive ions), and from 7-14, alkalinity (negative ions). All energy is alkaline, while waste is acidic (it burns!). See batteries for reference. Acids burn and dehydrate, while alkaloids soothe and relax. No extreme is ideal though, as balance is always the answer to achieve sustainability. However, balance does not necessarily mean the exact middle point, or a 50-50 distribution. We know the pH of our blood is around 7.4, and not 7.0, and the golden ratio of 1.618 permeates most patterns in nature, allowing for a fractal distribution and continuity, energetic efficiency, harmony, and aesthetic pleasantness. This ratio is also vastly present in the proportions of our human bodies. I highly recommend checking Dan Winter's work for further information down this rabbit hole, the power of bliss and the connections between our health, our heart, our emotions and electromagnetic fields.

There won't be an answer or firm stance regarding the cooked vs raw foods discussion in this book, nor about vegan vs paleo, but I'll raise a few points for reflection. I find it worth contemplating how the sun already "cooks" (charges, gives life to) fruits and plants to the point of perfection, while most living things that are touched by "human fire" end up destroyed. We all know what happens to our bodies when we are exposed to sunlight, and we all know what would happen to our bodies if they were exposed to fire. But we also know what is likely to happen to a pale person who's continually exposed to the sun for days in a row, or especially around 11-2 pm; and also what would happen to someone who's in a freezing climate and starts a campfire.

The only animals that present behavioral problems and dis-eases similar to humans are those what are domesticated and also consume cooked, processed foods. No animal in nature cooks their food or eats outside their species specific diet. Some people claim cooking our food is what allowed our brains to increase in size and evolve, while others claim cooking our food is exactly what caused the downfall of mankind, from some sort of Golden Age we used to live in. Until someone fasts for a considerable period of time and cleanses their vessel, they are not really qualified to determine what is optimal for themselves and what isn't.

If one consumes something that isn't whole, or in harmony, is it that much of a surprise that the person itself will become, to a certain degree, broken, fragmented, or dis-eased? It is not about saying which foods are good and which foods are bad, as that has always been, and always will be, a matter of choice, based on what someone wishes to experience. It is about finding ways of doing what we deem we must while making sure not to disrupt our internal balance. In other words, living in tune with our own particular nature, rather than acting foolishly according to our own caprice.

"He who lives in harmony with himself lives in harmony with the universe."
- 	*Marcus Aurelius*

We are not living in harmony with ourselves when our lifestyle results in accumulation of waste inside of our bodies. There are different degrees of constipation, however. There is the case of ingested toxins (acidic substances) that are isolated in mucus so they don't harm (burn) our healthy cells, as well as inorganic material or sediment, which could be referred to as lymphatic or cellular constipation. And there is the constipation of our intestinal tract, resulting from the ingestion of foods that have a long bowel transit time, are sticky and gluey, improper combinations, too frequent consumption, or too large portions. Usually a combination of all of the previous. What happens is that this is mostly a slow, gradual process, as bits of residue stick to the walls of our intestines and are left behind over time. As the consumption never stops, they keep accumulating, just like any pipe gets its walls dirty over the years, and sometimes gets clogged up altogether, if not periodically cleansed.

For reference, the total surface area of our small intestines has been determined to be about 250 square meters - the size of a tennis court. Recent studies suggest it may be "only" 32 square meters, however. Gotta love how reliable scientific studies and papers are... Which is another reason why I'll always favor facts learned through my own experience. Either way, it is worth doing a quick study of the characteristics and shape of our intestines, as well as the function of each of our digestive organs. If 32 square meters were covered by a thin layer of dust, can you imagine the volume of it when put together?

Being very conservative in my assumption,

we'll consider that most people eat 2 large meals a day, as well as 1 or 2 small ones. Simultaneously, the majority of people only visit the toilet once a day, and often less. And we all observe that, as people "age", they tend to develop protruding bellies. Is it obvious yet? As stated before, our breathing rate is a sign of life… but a full and dense belly isn't. That is, unless you're a pregnant woman. And that's exactly the issue… Most people over 30 walk around as if they were pregnant! Not only that, but we also have very large people walking around now. What most people consider a "normal" or "acceptable" belly, is not normal at all. I'll give a hint… those are not beer bellies, and much less "fat" resulted from an excess of "calories". Those are bellies full of undigested, dried, hardened feces, often decades old.

Some can easily accept these statements, some cannot, and others may think I'm simply exaggerating. After a week into consuming only juices or water, and especially beyond 21 days, the truth becomes obvious. Remember that substances lose volume when they're dehydrated, and they can stick to little crevices, or the organs themselves may bloat in order to accommodate them. Don't we get amazed at the amount of dust we find in our own houses after cleaning all of its surfaces?

In fact, many clues lie hidden in plain sight, for example, in our daily expressions. If someone "feels like shit", "smells like shit", or "looks like shit"... do we really have to put in so much effort, and even visit so-called experts, in an attempt to figure out the reason? The truth is most people are indeed full of shit, and not only in a metaphorical sense. Seems intriguing that over the course of all the years of "study" required in order to become a doctor, it's somehow forgotten to be mentioned that the father of medicine stated the following, over 2500 years ago:

"All disease starts in the gut."

"It is more important to know what sort of person has a disease than to know what sort of disease a person has."

"Illnesses do not come upon us out of the blue. They are developed from small daily sins against Nature. When enough sins have accumulated, illnesses will suddenly appear."

"If someone wishes for good health, one must first ask oneself if he is ready to do away with the reasons for his illness."

"Foolish is the doctor who despises the knowledge acquired by the ancients."

"If you are not your own doctor, you are a fool."

"Natural forces within us are the true healers of disease."
   -   *Hippocrates*

I guess those would be bad for business, huh. The 3rd quote in particular is one of the main reasons for confusion. It takes time, sometimes years, and often decades, for significant symptoms of one's poor food choices to manifest in a way that catches people's attention. Meanwhile, we're taught to believe that the alarm system of the body (pains, colds, flus, headaches, fevers, acne…) is not an actual alarm system, just like cars have in their panel, but only a malfunctioning that happens as a result of being exposed to different environments, such as changes of weather, being under the rain, or being "attacked by germs and bacteria".

Then, drugs are taken in order to *suppress* these symptoms, and not to address their cause. Essentially, they turn off the alarm, but don't put out the fire. Alas, the drugs themselves create an illusion of the problem being fixed, while only increasing the internal state of constipation and chaos. It turns out that *some* doctors are nothing but drug dealers with a college degree, and their true field of expertise is performing magic acts.

The top 3 causes of death in the United States are cancers, cardiovascular and respiratory problems, and medical error.

Colds and flus are a means of eliminating the accumulated toxins by literally expelling the excess of mucus that's built up. Acne and rashes are when the body attempts to do so via the skin... and so on. In truth, there are no hereditary diseases either... but there are hereditary food preferences.

Complicated dis-ease names can be understood as place in the body + inflammation (itis) and the degree of tissue degeneration. It basically tells us which part of the body is suffering the most from constipation. There is a superficial inflammation, which are acute and subacute states (the alarm system), a chronic state (things such as asthma, "autoimmune diseases", arthritis, and other recurring problems), which is either inherited by preconditioned genes or developed over many years and decades, and a degenerative state (cancers and such), when the malfunctioning reaches the point of turning into decay.

When the alarm system is suppressed, these toxins are buried deeper inside of our bodies, given the lack of opportunity to eliminate them. The human body is extremely intelligent, so it tends to gather and isolate these in specific locations, often close to lymph nodes, which would be akin to septic tanks. All inflammation is a problem of acidosis, which is why there are rashes, burning, dehydration, stiffness and pain involved. The worse the situation, the lower the pH of these acids become, until we "suddenly and mysteriously" end with something like a tumor, which is nothing but a pocket of highly acidic waste. Yea sure, let's do a biopsy and poke that thing to see what it is... "oh no, the cancer is now spreading!" *No shit, huh.* Another common development is the removal of a lymph node, together with all the waste that was being "handled" there. Sure fixes the short-term disturbance... but I wouldn't say that's the brightest idea when we think long-term instead. Would one consider getting rid of a clogged toilet altogether and leaving their house without it rather than... stop using it for a while in order to unclog it?

Those different levels of toxicity and degeneration can partially be seen by the color and the smell of mucus one expels. The deeper you get into a fast, the more common it will be to cough or sneeze out yellow-greenish mucus, sometimes incredibly thick, and even very small solids. Some people on the journey of healing themselves from so-called "incurable diseases" even report brown and black phlegm coming out of them.

Once a certain threshold of toxicity is ensured via the suppression of acute and subacute symptoms, the body will stop attempting to purge so often and will start compromising the efficiency of organs and systems to simply extend life as long as possible. That's why we see the alarm system being triggered so often in children and teenagers, while not so much in adults, who begin to present the issues related to chronic and degenerative states. When we begin seeing children and even babies with those later stages of malfunction and decay, we get an idea of how much un-working will be necessary to heal *generations* of trauma. Jabs *might* also be responsible for many of the issues in our little ones.

When there is suffocation on a cellular level, it means the blood (liquid life) is unable to reach them, so that group of cells, and in later stages whole organs, begin to decay. The increasing amount of toxins and acids stored inside of us, neutralized by mucus (often referred to as fat), slowly dehydrate ourselves. In a sense, mucus or fat is in no way a problem, but rather a symptom of toxicity. In fact, they are precisely what keeps people alive.

As babies, we are born extremely soft and flexible, reportedly at about 75% water (just like the planet, and most fruits). Apparently that number drops to around 60% for most adults, and as low as 50% for our elder citizens, who are brittle, stiff and wrinkled. In a nutshell, most human life seems to be a journey of a grape turning into a raisin.

However, that is not the effect of how many solar revolutions one has witnessed, or the passage of time in general, but of how one's daily actions, and mostly food preferences, gradually dehydrate their bodies, which culminates in the average lifespan of 72 years. From this perspective, most people are actually committing a very slow suicide. How long could humans actually live, still in a state of good health and vitality, if we remembered how to live in accordance to our own nature? On official record, the oldest person to have lived was a chinese man called Li Ching-Yuen, who passed the 250 years old mark and consumed mainly water and herbs.

"Man is born gentle and weak; at his death he is hard and stiff. All things, including the grass and the trees, are soft and pliable in life; dry and brittle in death. Stiffness is thus a companion of death; flexibility a companion of life."

-    *Lao Tzu*

This may be a more contradictory subject than diet itself, but since I'm sharing my own experience rather than trying to please or convince people, I must address how sodium chloride, commonly known as table salt, or simply salt, is the main culprit behind dehydration. If one believes in nutrition theory, then our bodies need *organic sodium*, from plant sources such as celery and other vegetables, algaes, or perhaps fish and other animals. Inorganic salt, which is essentially a rock, or dirt, is not only useless to the human body, but poisonous. Aside from appearance, there is another thing that sodium chloride, refined sugar, refined flours and cocaine have in common: they are all isolated, refined, highly stimulant substances - in other words, drugs. And those fancy variations with different colours are no better, for the record. Our bodies do need sodium, potassium, and other salts to function, that is true, but we require the *organic* variation.

While we're at it, if there's anything one is unable to consume without adding sodium chloride to it... do we even like its taste to begin with? It's not that different from people who can only drink coffee with a lot of sugar in it. And if we were to eliminate sodium chloride altogether... what "foods" would be left that could still be eaten and appreciated without its addiction? After all, would anyone consider drinking sea water when thirsty?

If someone drinks several litres of water at once, they may be superficially hydrated, or even over-hydrated... but there is such a thing as a chronic state of dehydration, which is caused by the accumulated toxins, acids and filth mentioned before. Those cannot be eliminated in a day, or even in weeks. It is a gradual process, as they are very dried and stuck to our insides, so they must be slowly rehydrated in order to be successfully eliminated.

Gradually, the accumulated mucus causes separation between the cells of our body, eventually muffling the communication between tissues and even organs. This creates separation and noise (scrambled vibrations) within ourselves. People are confused because their own cells can't communicate efficiently with each other. The mucus and filth eventually makes people literally and metaphorically dense.

As inner communication deteriorates... outer communication follows suit. People begin to perceive separation between themselves and other groups of people... People begin to separate their skin from the environment with clothes... People begin to further separate themselves from the sun with chemicals and sunglasses... Now people are further separating themselves from not just who they perceive as different, but from literally everyone else... And at last, people are creating an external barrier between themselves and the very air that keeps us alive. All the perceived mess in the world is just a reflection of the mess inside of ourselves. People harm themselves... which results in external acts of violence. To live backwards is to be evil.

Or, maybe this was all just a tale of fiction to entertain the reader... I'm not claiming to be right, nor to have all the answers. And it's not as if one would go about believing some strangers' words just because a third stranger said they're qualified to speak about it, *right*? It is worth remembering that businesses *need* returning customers, otherwise they'd go bankrupt. Someone who really has your best interests in mind will empower you in such a way that you never bother them again! After all, they have their own lives and dreams to fulfill... babysitting is only fun up to a certain degree. Finding the truth is ultimately a DIY project - just like living.

Nothing will be solved without addressing the root of the problems, that is, returning to what's natural: in alignment with life; self sustaining; intelligent. Just like water slowly erodes rocks, we use liquids to dissolve the resistance (debris from food and inorganic material) so the circuits of our body become unobstructed and the breath, energy, or life force, flows freely again.

Abusing our sensory organs gradually makes us numb, requiring greater stimulants in order to feel something. Fasting, or returning to a state of inner silence and purity, is the only way to fully reclaim our sensitivity. Then we'll be equipped to actually see for ourselves the effects of each thing (energy, or vibration) we consume. Without a clear, unbiased perspective, we can't even trust ourselves... let alone others.

If we consider being in a state of chronic inflammation, dehydration and pain, akin to living in hell, it could be said the healthy individual lives in heaven. One is in a perpetual state of suffering and attempting to escape from it, literally burning from the inside out, while the other lives in a peace that permeates through all aspects of their being. Therefore, fasting is essentially going through purgatory. While falling from heaven to hell is a quick trip, one cannot avoid going through purgatory when climbing from hell to heaven. Only by eliminating all of the accumulated toxins and filth (sins), will one be allowed (allow themselves) to step into the gates of heaven (enter into a different realm of living).

Do humans age, or do we dry up?

4. IN ORDER TO

"There has never been, and cannot be, a good life without self-control."
-       *Leo Tolstoy*

Although they tend to be centered around some aspect of health, there are many reasons that can lead someone to fast, and a vast range of benefits that come from doing so. If you can control what you put in your mouth, you can control all other aspects of your life. In my opinion, self-mastery will always be the highest benefit one will attain through fasting.

Going along with the analogy from the last section, if one is "living in hell", or in an inflamed body, it would only be natural to have the company of "demons" instead of "angels". That is how I perceive parasites to be.

In literature, we have demons, or vampires, as beings who drink humans' blood, are able to manipulate them through hypnosis, are often pale, hide from the sun, and are weak against garlic, wood, silver, and God's presence. However, vampires are unable to enter someone's house without the owner's permission, and demons often form a pact with humans where they deliver promises of satisfying earthly desires in exchange for decades of one's life.

Translating... Parasites feed not only on the trash we consume, but also on our blood and vital force. They induce cravings by manipulating us via the connection between our gut and our brain. They hide in our intestines, and die when exposed to sunlight (after being expelled from our insides). Garlic is a well known anti-parasitic, as well as certain wood barks, such as cascara sagrada, and also colloidal silver. God's presence means the awareness of our true self - when we consciously inhabit our body and stop making excuses. At last, they cannot enter our bodies (temples) unless we invite them inside through our food choices and the cultivation of an inner terrain that is suitable for their living. To be baptized by water would be akin to water fasting, while an exorcism is what I call doing an enema.

However, it is a misconception to view microbes, bacteria and parasites as enemies, or evil entities that attack us. These beings are the decomposers and scavengers of nature, which means their job is to break down decaying organic matter which will in turn become fertilizer for new life to arise - the never ending cycle of nature. If they are inside of us... there must be something rotting! In fact, we would probably die much faster without them helping process the garbage inside of us.

We could also compare them to rats and roaches, who enter our house when we forget to take out the trash. They are not there to harm us... they only want to eat the trash! It should be common sense that getting rid of them while refusing to take out the trash will only result in them coming back again and again... Or, we could also say that they are the smoke, but neither the fire nor its fuel. A simple matter of cause and effect. Since they are present in the crime scene, it's certainly convenient to shift the blame to them! After all, the best lies stick as close as possible to the truth.

We don't have an "immune system" either. We have a series of response mechanisms that deal with removing foreign material and maintaining homeostasis. We can adapt to things (either through compromising or strengthening), but there's no such thing as immunity.

Most people are familiar with Louis Pasteur's Germ Theory... But to blindly believe it without even researching Antoine Bechamp's Terrain Theory is both foolish and reckless.

"It is the mark of an educated mind to be able to entertain a thought without accepting it."
- *Aristotle*

Again, the issue arises from overloading and accumulation. Over time, parasites and bacteria make themselves at home and start spreading to all areas of the body, slowly taking over control of it - though in reality all they're doing is decomposing someone who's already slowly killing themselves. They're also the source of many of our desires, and when we ask ourselves "what do I feel like eating", they are the ones who answer.

Gods and Goddesses don't have cravings... Parasites do.

The good news is that a refinement of our eating habits is all that it takes for them to gradually move away on their own - though fasting, certain herbs or aged orin can greatly speed up the process. If one's living life mostly unconsciously, it's like their body is an abandoned house. After getting so cozy inside of us without even paying rent or being disturbed, parasites may need a little incentive to be evicted, just like a lazy tenant who began to think that they own the place. Even if they are not necessarily a threat, it is still necessary for us to reclaim the territory inside our bodies with our awareness, in order to allow our true identity to be fully manifested and expressed.

Speaking of desires, there is a strong tie between our eating habits and how we deal with our emotions. From an early age, we are often taught to be distracted, or suppress our feelings in general, as well as receive rewards for behaving in an expected way, through the consumption of foods, namely sweets and other treats. Most parties, family gatherings and celebrations are also centered around eating. And nowadays, it is also very common to be eating while watching something, whether it be in the cinema, on our phones, or the television. There is a gradual but consistent process of associating different foods with different emotions. Food essentially becomes an emotional crutch.

Just like there is physical constipation, water retention and inability of crying can be associated with emotional constipation, when one has difficulties in expressing their feelings, while mostly burying them inside. As the intestines get filled and the breathing capacity impaired, mental and spiritual (remember spirit means breath) constipation are also developed. All aspects of our being are always interconnected in one way or another. We cannot separate our physical life from our spiritual life.

That's one of the reasons why crying (emotional detox), sweating, taking a shower, entering natural bodies of water or getting under the rain can be so relaxing and refreshing. The flowing water allows us to release stored emotions, and this is just as much of an important part of the healing process as any other.

Through fasting, one has the opportunity of confronting their current situation without relying on foods for distraction or suppression. In fact, I dare say most of our eating is actually emotional eating, and not out of true hunger or necessity. We eat to cope with our current situations, difficulties and stress - or to reward ourselves in some way. When we remove that option, we are forced to take inventory of our lives.

Even leaving all healing aside, I highly recommend anyone to, at least once in their lives, consider doing a 2-3 days water fast while also dismissing contact with other people and the internet. Just you and a notebook; maybe in nature, maybe in your apartment, it doesn't really matter. Be alone with yourself and learn to be comfortable with it. Most people aren't, and eating, or using drugs, are common ways of escaping from ourselves - which is only an illusion, since that cannot truly be done.

All one can do is sacrifice their awareness and live in a constant state of unconsciousness and indulgence on distractions. When we turn off the distractions and the noise, we find ourselves in silence, or peace, which is the natural state of existence. When we explore and acknowledge all aspects of ourselves, we learn to abide in that space of neutrality, without being constantly shaken by the perpetual change of circumstances around us. If we don't learn to connect with, accept and be with ourselves as individuals who are already whole, we will always struggle to do so with other people, since we will be always looking for someone to fix or complete us, rather than complement and multiply.

Fasting is a wonderful opportunity to connect, or re-connected, with the core of our being, perform self examination, and reflect on the life we've been leading, as well as contemplating what is actually important, and what's been engaged simply out of habit or external pressure. Who are we really, and what do we really want to make out of this experience? If we don't center ourselves from time to time, we risk getting lost in the storm.

This also ties into spiritual purposes or biblical fasting, as the cleaner our body becomes, the easier it is to get in touch with our intuition, or maybe some may consider it a way of connecting with [God*]. Quite a number of people seem to have done 40 days or more of fasting, either in the desert or in caves, and came back with amazing insights and revelations... It certainly increases our sensitivity, and allows us to slow down and pay attention to the little details we often miss in the hurry of daily life.

*whenever you read God, feel free to substitute it to whatever you deem most appropriate, such as

Nature, Tao, Goddess, the Universe, Great Spirit, the divine, higher self, angels, ancestors, elementals, etc. They're all different terms that point to that which is beyond words to begin with.

Not only our minds are much clearer as we clean our intestines, but that also results in an innate feeling of interconnectedness with all life around us. I've also experienced animals approaching me differently during a fast, as well as babies and children in general. It's like they know you have "stepped into another dimension", or are hooked on something special. It's common sense they're more sensitive to energy. Not to mention how synchronicities sky-rocket. These results get deeper, better and more mysterious with each passing week, and are almost immediately halted, or at least considerably lessened, the moment we take a bite of something.

Fasting can also be approached as a way of transitioning into different lifestyles, whether that be dropping addictions, changing your daily routine, healing from a broken relationship, entering into a new season, adopting a new diet, and so on. By simply doing something like a 48-72 hours water fast, or perhaps 7 days of juice fasting, we will attain a degree of clarity of mind, clearer skin, a soft reset of our taste buds, the elimination of our most recent meals, and an overall healing of our whole being. It basically disrupts the momentum we had going in all aspects, and therefore allows us to create something new in its place. For that, however, one must actually make new, different decisions after breaking the fast, instead of simply returning to their old lives and habits out of custom and convenience. It facilitates, not determines, the transition. Our actions always have the final say.

It is worth mentioning that besides its healing potential, water fasting could also be seen as a way of reducing expenses, whether that be taking on intermittent fasting and eating less on a daily basis, or adopting the habit of doing one or a few days of water fasting every month. Word of caution: remember to only fast to the degree you feel inspired and willing to, while avoiding extreme measures of all kinds. Don't push your own limits unless you know what you're getting yourself into, and have a good reason for doing so. Otherwise rather than healing something, one would only be developing an eating disorder.

Of course, by healing yourself you'll also save up on many future medical bills, since a (truly) healthy individual has no reason to visit a doctor other than for emergencies, such as in the case of physical accidents, broken bones and similar (rare) situations.

If we were to continue living in the same, or even in a higher state of health and vitality, while eating less, that is, requiring less external inputs, wouldn't we have become more efficient? There may be people starving in certain regions of the world, but in most countries, people are suffering from over indulgence, and not for a lack of resources.

"Real wealth and freedom consists in a minimum of needs."

- *Epicurus*

Most people like eating. Therefore, to willingly decide to stop eating for a period of time, as already mentioned, is a wonderful way of training our minds and developing self-discipline, or as I prefer to call it, self-mastery. It is a wonderful opportunity to take a minimalistic or simple lifestyle to another dimension, and really put into perspective how much of our lives are actual needs, and how much are only wants. If you feel you cannot live without something, aren't you restricting and limiting yourself? I find it best to appreciate what's available, while avoiding becoming too attached or dependent on it, as the only permanent aspect of life is impermanence. We can have, but never possess. That goes for physical things, habits, beliefs, and also relationships.

I also consider fasting a great tool for developing humility and patience, which in turn allows us to appreciate the natural pleasures of life even more. Other suggestions for taking this process to another level, that one may contemplate engaging in either a temporary or permanent basis: daily meditation or any other similar practice that appeals to you, sleeping on the floor (or on a yoga mat, thin cushion, or even a futon), taking cold showers in the morning, not using air conditioning or heating, not looking oneself in the mirror, not using makeup, completely ignoring customary beliefs, always being spontaneous while remaining respectful and considerate of others, acting and living your life without a single care for what other people think of you, and treating everyone you meet as if they were already a dear friend, regardless of whether or not you like them in the first place. Love yourself, love your life, and love everything and everyone you meet. Learn to accept things as they are, and to respond consciously to them rather than re-acting unconsciously. Simply dismiss what you don't want to remain in your experience, and do what you, deep down, feel is right for every moment.

The less we resist life, the less effort is required to live. The more we appreciate life, the more our lives are appreciated. We create our own value by choosing to be a creator of our own dreams, instead of a reactor to other people's.

5. CONSCIOUS INTERMITTENT FASTING

"The cave you fear to enter holds the treasure you seek."

- *Joseph Campbell*

You may skip this section if you already eat only once or twice a day, or if you consider it optimal for yourself to have small but frequent meals throughout the day.

As stated before, we all fast unconsciously every night for around 8 hours... which is how we keep living even amidst all the abuse we put our bodies through. Would anyone question the amount of physical, emotional and mental healing that takes place during our sleep hours?

Many people naturally avoid a meal in the morning, or avoid eating too much too late at night, which extends this period. While on the other hand, we have those who can't go more than an hour or two without munching on something, and even wake up in the middle of the night to do so. Just between us, that sounds more like an addiction than a necessity. There are a lot of large people and there are a lot of old people... but there are not a lot of large, old people. Folks that live to advanced ages - in comparison to the average lifespan - usually don't eat much.

In fact, this is already in the realm of scientific research, for those who care about such things. The only known way of increasing the lifespan of mice is to decrease their food consumption. The whole array of benefits from intermittent fasting and even water fasting for up to 24-72 hours can be found with little research. It basically boosts our vitality and metabolism in all levels.

As amazing as fasting for 3 or more days at a time may be, what you're doing for the rest of the year is just as important, if not more. Experimenting with intermittent fasting is way less daunting than going over a day without chewing something, and can serve as a bridge between the two. Especially if you treat the meals later in the day as a sort of reward, or delayed gratification system - you'll begin to earn them. When you already start your day eating, you're already directing blood and energy towards digestion, which means your brain and muscles won't work as efficiently. As far as I'm concerned, eating anything heavy in the morning is the biggest sabotage one can do against themselves, as it will compromise the rest of their day.

I'll lay a suggestion of how to approach this based on my experience.

"Adapt what is useful, reject what is useless, and add what is specifically your own."
-     *Bruce Lee*

Let's take an average person that sleeps from 23:00 to 6:00, has a morning meal at 7:00, lunch at 13:00 and dinner at 19:00, as well as snacks in between. Intermittent fasting doesn't necessarily mean eating less, only less often - although it can be both. We could begin by making sure the first meal consists of only fruits, and gradually liquefy it into smoothies, juices, and eventually only tea or coffee (without sweeteners).

I would also suggest turning any snacks (non large or main meals) into fresh fruit, or a mix of nuts, seeds and dried fruit. Avoid consuming high protein foods and starch or sweets in the same meal, as those two don't digest well together, given their requirements of enzymes of opposing pH. Pick one and have it alone, with vegetables or a salad. Fruits should be consumed by themselves, and not as a dessert, given their quick digestion time - otherwise they will end up fermenting on top of the meal. Avoid drinking up to half an hour before your larger meals and 30 to 60 minutes afterwards, otherwise you'd be diluting your gastric juices. Chew your solids into liquids, and also "chew" your liquids in order to properly mix them with saliva. It is best to not have distractions or stress around you during eating times, and rather eat with mindfulness, being fully present and savoring each bite. *How* we eat is just as important as *what* we eat.

Great rewards come from researching ayurveda and traditional chinese medicine, understanding the specifics of your body, any present imbalances, and realizing for yourself, through trial and error, which foods are agreeable to you and which aren't, as well as how to adapt to the seasons, climate and region, stage of life, and how to use the correct herbs and spices for your best advantage.

Now your first meal, or breakfast, that is, breaking the (night) fast, would be a fruit snack around 9 or 10. You could continue to push this until you're not eating anything before lunch, anywhere between 11 and 14. If deemed necessary, you could increase your lunch and dinner portions, as well as the size of an afternoon snack. It would be optimal to also not eat too late at night, since it is ideal to sleep without food in your stomach, say 2 to 4 hours between your last bite and going to bed. It pays off to learn about the circadian cycle and the organ clock from chinese medicine.

We basically made it to a 16:8 intermittent fasting window, which means we fast for 16 hours (counting sleep) and then only eat during the following 8 hours. One could be having lunch at noon, a fruit and/or nuts snack around 4 pm and then dinner at 7-8 pm. From my experience, the benefits further increased when I ditched the snack and kept to only two meals, around 1-2 pm and 6-7 pm, making it a 18:6 or even 20:4 fasting to eating window. Alternatively, you could drink juice through the afternoon, or between lunch and dinner. The mental clarity you have in the morning begins to be noticeable and your body slowly adapts, to the point if you ever decide to eat early in the day again, you'll immediately notice your performance dropping. It's been years since I last felt hungry before 2-4 pm.

For those who resonate with a raw vegan lifestyle, this is a wonderful opportunity to become about 50% raw, given that you turn your lunch into a fruit only meal or a salad, and then have your cooked foods later in the day. You could do the opposite, since our digestive power is at its highest around noon... but in my experience it pays off to be "lighter" through the day and leave the heavier meal to the end of its activities.

It also would be beneficial to keep the most unhealthy (from the reader's perspective) food choices to the weekend, or at least to later in the day. If you're going to have them anyway, at least do so in a responsible, balanced way... and craft a system where you "earn" them, rather than indulging at every opportunity or excuse. The less you "cheat", the less you're actually cheating yourself... and the more satisfying the occasional splurge will be.

Remember that if you're seeking desserts, you're probably stressed in some way. Paraphrasing Emerson, our health is our most important wealth, and we gain the strength of the temptations we choose to ignore. The healthier one becomes, the healthier their "cheats" will be as well. This happens through the refinement and reclamation of sensitivity of our taste buds - do a 3 days water fast and you'll have the most delicious fruit you've had in years.

The apex of this lifestyle came to me, and many others, in the realization of OMAD - although most people will say u-mad... It stands for one meal a day, which translates into 22-23 fasting hours to a 1 or 2 hours eating window. It is almost as if one is doing one day fasts on a daily basis, going through all their day, work activities and exercises while reaping the benefits of not having to stop and digest food... and then you reward yourself with a large meal in the evening, when nothing other than leisure or chilling with the family will be requested of you before retiring to bed.

At first it might be easier to allow the drinking of coconut water or juices through the day, maybe even a few pieces of fruits if necessary - which are my recommendation to anyone that feels they need to consume something before their next meal. This is as far as one gets to receiving the benefits from fasting while still chewing foods on a daily basis.

After a whole day of being empty, almost anything will taste delicious, which can also help with making optimal choices. If that isn't the case, even not so healthy foods will more or less get a pass, since you're giving your body over 20 hours to deal with it. There are *many* metabolic benefits from this lifestyle, and if one gets used to it, stepping into 1-3 days fasts also becomes much easier.

6. TYPES

There are different "protocols" that are regarded as different types of fasting. In my opinion, dry fasting is fasting, while in all others scenarios we are still consuming something through our mouths... But for convenience, we'll set that aside, and simply look at them as different densities of living, or levels of detoxification, through the ladder that leads to health. And health, or being whole, is not about following specific diets, or adding anything in particular to your grocery list... it is about removing what no longer serves your current (or desired) state of being. It is not an act of creation or building, but that of sculpting.

Something that anyone can do, and dare I say most people should, is to fast from a single (or a few) things for any period of time, although in this case I would say at least a month in order to notice a perceptible change and attain a new perspective. It could be dairy, gluten, grains in general, animal products, fried foods, weed, alcohol, refined sugar, processed foods... Simply pick anything you either know it's unhealthy or are over the fence given people sharing different opinions about it… and put it to test yourself. After a month without it, you will be qualified to decide whether your life is better with or without it, that is, if the pleasure from indulging in it trumps the efforts from having your body process and eliminate it.

A most simple and easy way to "fast" would be eating only one type of food, such as rice, or any other grain or legume porridge-soup style, with minimal seasoning and in small portions. For most people coming from a conventional diet, doing this for a week would prove to considerably help with the elimination of recent waste and also give the body a short rest, as well as developing a certain degree of self control. Just from eliminating junk, fried, processed, refined and animal foods in general, one will feel a great difference in energy levels. Focusing on only one food will ease the digestive burden, regardless of what it is, and allow a soft reset of the taste buds. All following types of fasting will increase these benefits exponentially, and add many more.

Another option would be having only blended vegetable soups instead, with both being wonderful ways to do a gentle (albeit superficial) cleanse during winter, while still keeping oneself warm and with the feeling of being nourished. Ever stopped to think why these are acceptable dishes to feed a "sick" person or an elder whose health is compromised?

A superior version of the previous would be to consume only raw fruits for any length of time, or focus on only one type, which is also known as a "fruit island". This way you're providing your body with plenty of hydration and fiber content, which will promote a deep cleanse for most people. The more astringent the chosen fruits, the deeper the detox. Doing so for one or more weeks, especially during spring or summer, is a wonderful way to adjust to the weather and bear with the heat, while experimenting a fruitarian or raw vegan lifestyle for a while. You'll be light, refreshed and filled with energy.

Fruits have about the same percentage of water as we do, and they neither run from us nor develop chemicals to turn them poisonous - they have bright, beautiful colours and a sweet aroma when ripe, all in order to invite us in. It is not a coincidence - we have a symbiotic relationship with fruit trees. It is also a great thing to do for a few days before entering a liquid fast.

In the realm of fruit islands, watermelons, grapes, oranges, mangoes or bananas are the most common ones - but pick whatever is in season and catches your attention. I for one wouldn't mind being stranded on a deserted tropical island, so long as there are coconuts!

Next we consider an all-liquids fast, which would include anything juiced or blended, going from juices, to smoothies, nut and seed milks, or even vegetable broth and soups. Now your digestive system has to work way less than before, as the food consumed is already "pre-chewed". This is a wonderful state to live in, since the detox won't be as deep as to cause much unpleasantness, but will most certainly promote a noticeable degree of healing over time. If cars work perfectly fine on liquid fuel, why wouldn't we? On a daily basis, if you are eating, I highly recommend making the first meal a juice or smoothie, or, next best, fruit, while leaving the heavier and cooked foods for later.

It is incredibly easy, although potentially messy, to make "milk" with any nut or seed - my favorites being almond, cashews, hazelnuts and sunflower seeds. All you need is a large bowl, a blender and a cheesecloth to strain it. Wash your seeds well and soak them overnight, wash it again and then use a 1:3 (from the volume of when they were dry) ratio to water, or add little by little until you achieve the desired consistency.

There are many other options to play with, such as pumpkin seeds, sesame seeds, hemp, macadamia, walnuts, coconut... A good way to increment it would be to add a sweetener of choice, or a handful of raisins or dates. You can also use some cacao powder and cinnamon or vanilla for taste. Alternatively, after having the "milk", you can use it as a base for other smoothies.

Speaking of smoothies, the fruits, berries and spice combinations are endless, so I'll leave only a personal favorite "cheat" of mine, that especially if you've been raw or on liquids only for a while, should make you completely forget about any cravings for desserts. Freeze overripe bananas for at least 24 hours, and get your hands on fresh coconut water. Soak a bunch of raisins and/or a few dates on the coconut water in the fridge, to cool it a little. Then blend by themselves or with cacao powder, cinnamon powder and (optional) peanut butter. You can also add berries or something like spirulina if you're so inclined. I'll leave out the ratios because I highly recommend you blend little by little to achieve the taste and consistency that fits yourself... but it's pretty much a healthy, heavenly "milkshake" kind of thing!

With juice feasting we are removing the fibers and pretty much any digestive effort that was still being requested of the body, so the healing and detoxification will be taken to a new level - I would say they're increased by an order of magnitude from now on. Due to the high volume of juices ingested, most people will experience an abundance of energy, as it would be almost impossible to consume that same amount of fruits and vegetables, on a daily basis, by chewing them. The high volume of liquids will also make it easier to hydrate and loosen up mucus and accumulated filth in the colon, and ease up any cravings by literally keeping you occupied drinking juice all day!

The most common and affordable choices tend to be watermelons in spring and summer, and oranges or grapes in autumn and winter. Other melons, apples, pineapples and mandarins are also great, and while it is wise to use the seasonal and regional availability as a guideline, don't let that become a limitation... go with whatever's ripe, tasty, affordable and calling out to you. I've had both streaks of 10+ days consuming only one type of fruit, as well as weeks where every day I'd go with a different one... though in general, I found it easier to have only one type of juice per day. An amusing idea, especially if one is going for only a week, and has any inclination towards yoga or meditation, would be to have each day juices of the color of a specific chakra, going from the root upwards (ROYGBIV) - though the options would be very limited for the last 3 days, grape juice is known for being one of the most potent cleansers and detoxifiers.

I'm particularly more drawn to fruit juices than vegetables, but many recommend including both, especially if you're in a cold season or going for a long duration. My favorite vegetable juices are apple-celery-parsley and pineapple-kale-lemon, but just like smoothies, the possible combinations and recipes on the internet are endless. It is worth mentioning green juices are known for assisting with heavy metal detoxification; parsley and cilantro in particular. Carrot-spinach is allegedly effective in cleansing the digestive tract - if you can stomach it to begin with... Adjust the ratio of fruits or carrots to make it palatable to you and gradually change it as you get used to the flavour. From my experience, vegetable juices are quite a treat to have sometimes in the evening, but more time and resource demanding than fruit juices.

Most people would be drinking between 4 and 8 litres in a juice feast, often from morning to night. When we reduce that amount, I begin calling it a juice fast instead - where we would have anywhere from 1 to 3 litres of juices a day, sometimes diluted, and also (optional) distilled water and herbal teas. As beautiful as fresh juices may be, they are still an energizer to a certain degree - which is why they are most amazing for cleansing and up to a certain degree of healing, but only when we enter the realm of water and dry fasting will we be able to address the deepest traumas, scars and genetic predispositions.

The less you consume, the faster the body heals. It is not about one way being better or worse than another, but rather finding the speed of healing and elimination that matches your current state of being and lifestyle. For instance, the average person, simply by getting rid of dairy, gluten and changing their morning meal into only fruits or a green juice would already have their whole lives transformed... but if they jumped straight into a long fast, it might be too intense for them to handle, given the large amount of stored toxins. That's why I consider intermittent fasting and playing with fruits and juices so important, as they are the most gentle and efficient means of eliminating the recent garbage, and gradually begin to dig into deeper layers of tissue.

Unless you find yourself in a very degenerate state of health, and are willing to face the struggle of an 180º turn as soon as possible, there is absolutely no need to hurry, and nowhere to hurry to. Learn to enjoy the ups and downs of the process, since high and low depend on each other. Labels and numbers mean nothing in comparison to how much vitality you feel and how clear your mind is.

This in-between zone between juice feasting and distilled water only is to allow for a gentle transition, while still relying - although less and less, on something that tastes good and stimulates us in order to serve as motivation. It also helps us to gradually see how well the body can perform with progressively less dependence on external substances, and increase the contrast with what's considered "normal" or was previously accepted by the reader as an appropriate lifestyle. Most people have never experienced true health, so how would they know what they're missing?

Two options that provide a deeper cleanse than drinking juices, while still being considerably less intense than a water fast, would be drinking distilled water with lemon and a sweetener of choice, or fresh coconut water. One is perfect for colder seasons while the other is most wonderful to be done in spring or summer, especially if you're living in the tropics. Lemons are powerful detoxifiers, and drinking them with warm water will assist in dealing with the cold, which can sometimes be a problem when juice fasting - although easily solved by wearing more clothes. Coconut water not only is extremely refreshing, but also helps the functioning and regular movement of our digestive system. Coconuts take about 9 months to grow and ripen, which is just another reason why I'm so fascinated with them, and consider them to be the most optimal source of hydration for humans - after we outgrow our mother's milk. They are truly a gift of nature for anyone living in the tropics.

Both coconut water, celery juice and kelp powder have helped me ease any salt or savory cravings I've had during longer fasts.

When we move into the realm of (preferably distilled) water fasting, the healing and detox are again increased by another order of magnitude. Now there is no fructose or carbohydrates being ingested, no amino acids, no fats and no minerals. You are giving your body a complete vacation from food, which allows it to fully switch into autophagy and ketosis mode. The body begins to destroy and reutilize its weaker cells, as well as breaking down any "fat" deposits.

I highly recommend having cleansed most of your intestinal tract through either a raw food diet or a few weeks of juice fasting before venturing here, unless you're keeping it to under 3 days. Most people will need to also take a vacation from their work and some activities in order to dive in deeper than a week here, and you should really know what you're doing before you do so. The longer one has cleansed with fruits and juices, the easier it will be to shift into distilled water only - although staying in the realm of only 1-3 days at a time will already provide tremendous benefits. I recommend drinking as much as you're thirsty for, but in small sips, as to provide the necessary hydration to eliminate waste, but never flood the body. The less you drink, the closer you'll be to the realm of dry fasting.

Why distilled water? If inorganic minerals did us any good, we could go on living off rocks or the soil itself. Unless plant life has turned those into organic minerals, they are of no use to us. Therefore, anything other than distilled water is simply "dirty water", and that dirt gradually clogs up our insides, or at best considerably increases the burden of our organs of elimination. A most compelling reason is for those living in the city, where the water supply is laced with fluoride and chlorine on top of it all. Anyone who buys a water distiller machine and sees the dirt that is left on it won't dare to go back to their old ways. After some time drinking distilled water, tap or mineral water simply feels dirty or unpleasant to drink. Not trying to convince anyone though, as those who are willing will seek the truth through their own experience.

Distilled water is essentially clouds in liquid form, without any substance other than hydrogen and oxygen, making it the perfect solvent for us to cleanse our bodies with. Anything that doesn't belong inside will be washed away. On a side note, the juice of fruits and vegetables, as well as coconut water, may be considered a form of distilled water, since the plants go through the trouble of filtering and structuring it for us.

Especially when it's cold or in the beginning or end of the day, it is very helpful to have your water warm, as it will be more easily assimilated by the body. Some people put a piece of ginger in it, a few drops of lemon, or different herbs. If you know what you're doing, plain herbal teas can be a good addiction to water fasting during the cold months.

You can also play with leaving the distilled water under the sun or the moon, charge it with crystals or shungite, write affirmations on the glass or on a paper under it, leaving it close to tensor rings, etc. In fact, I highly recommend showing gratitude, love, or any other feeling deemed appropriate before consuming anything, especially during a fast. You don't have to say it out loud, or even put your hands together - our feelings always come from the heart. Also avoid drinking anything when you're upset for any reason; but see if you can recenter and calm yourself first.

At last, when we completely cease the consumption of any solids or liquids through our mouth, we are in fact fasting - dry fasting. Again the benefits and the depths of cleansing are raised by an order of magnitude, if not more, compared to distilled water fasting. And those continue to increase exponentially with each passing day. Now the body doesn't have the luxury of using the ingested water to hydrate and eliminate toxins, although most of our metabolic waste is eliminated through the lungs anyway, and some degree of water is still absorbed through our nose and skin.

What happens then is that our body takes the autophagy to another level - whichever cells are weak, damaged or unessential will be destroyed so its waters can be reutilized. Many will literally implode to turn into resources for the rest of the body. Allegedly, even waste itself will simply be burned off as the body naturally raises its temperature to purify itself. I have experienced what felt akin to a fever, and in a sense, I would compare it to what people do to themselves through extensive workouts. Maybe we could say it's a purification by fire, rather than washing away with water?

Anyone venturing into periods of over a day of dry fasting might consider thoroughly cleansing most of the sediment, mucus and waste from their bodies beforehand, through the use of juices or other forms of distilled water. In my experience, it certainly made dry fasting easier. Often when I'm deep into liquid fasting, I'll naturally be dry fasting until 3-5pm without even giving it a thought. Whenever I'm eating on a daily basis, especially cooked foods [still OMAD], I feel much more thirsty, and also earlier in the day, like noon-1 pm. Although there are people who, even in very unhealthy states, push through a few days of dry fasting and experience incredible results; while others would say it would be crazy to dive into dry fasting before doing a lot of cleansing with liquids first. Proceeding with caution would be most wise, but If you have fears or doubts, then you're not ready for it.

We don't die from the toxins themselves, but by how they clog up our bodies. If one jumps too fast into more advanced forms of fasting, I feel they can literally risk suffocating in their own waste. Everyone knows what usually happens when you try to climb the stairs too fast, or jump several steps at a time. Many are so constipated and dis-eased that it may be ideal to approach the porridge and soup styles of eating first, with intermittent water or dry fasting, as well as having many salads and green smoothies, and only then begin exploring periods of juice and water fasting.

In my opinion, the best approach to dry fasting is to start with intermittent dry fasting, say around 12 hours, and gradually climb up to 14, 16, 18, 20... It is a wonderful combination with any form of liquid fasting or OMAD, and simply doing this many hours on a daily basis already multiplies the so many benefits of the other modalities, in ways that cannot be expressed through words - one must feel it. After you can comfortably dry fast for 18-20 hours on a daily basis, you may begin to explore 24 and 36 hours periods. Remember to go much slower and carefully than with other types of fasting though, as things can get quite intense. And always break your dry fast period with small sips, never gulping down large volumes of fluids.

Anything beyond (I have many friends who have dry fasted regularly for a few days at a time, even up to 9 days at once) will be left for a future book, as I currently lack the necessary experience to talk about it. But hey, even "science" acknowledges that it takes at least 3 days for someone to die without ingesting water... so it's definitely "safe" to explore within this range.

Either way, I've already mentioned how dry fasting is true fasting, and anyone approaching this would do well to go by feeling rather than reading from a book. Don't let fear stop you, but don't be too reckless either... The good news is that if things get too intense, all you have to do is drink a few sips of something, such as warm distilled water or that from a fresh coconut, to halt the process. Just like eating some fruit or steamed vegetables will immediately halt the detox process during a liquid fast. In other words, ingesting anything more complex than what you are currently consuming (in the case of dry fasting, air and sunlight) will tell your body to tone down the cleansing in accordance to the density of what was consumed. Keep in mind not to shock your body though! More on how to break a fast properly in the After section.

A person who begins venturing into the realm of dry fasting is likely to no longer need assistance in regards to inner cleansing anyway, given how in tune they will be with their own body, cycles and intuition. It is a survival of the fittest scenario, and whatever cells remain afterwards, will be the best and healthier version of yourself.

"Simplicity is the ultimate sophistication."
-    *Leonardo da Vinci*

7. WHEN & WHERE

Short answer: here and now.

There will never be a better, and in fact, there won't ever be another time other than now. But especially if you're beginning to explore fasting, it is most sensible to find a period when you won't have to deal with much stress or demands, and can focus most of your attention on healing and resting. Especially upon venturing on a journey of small amounts of juices, water or dry, it is crucial to have the time and flexibility to care for yourself.

If you can't find ways of taking a vacation of sorts, I'd recommend intermittent fasting and OMAD most of all, doing short fasts more frequently, or perhaps going the fruit only or juice feasting route. It is a wonderful thing to get into the habit of fasting regularly, in whichever way is most agreeable to your current state, by introducing several short fasts "for maintenance" in between the larger ones. I'll lay a few examples.

One could choose to fast for one day every week. For instance, every Monday, following a potential splurge during the weekend. Or, alternatively, one could fast for two days every weekend, avoiding the aforementioned self-destruction and making it easier to adopt healthier choices during the 5 days of the week. For any religious person, you could take your Sabbath, Sunday or [...] and also fast on that day. You can also simply do spontaneous fasting, such as skipping meals when you don't really feel hungry or doing one to three days at any time deemed helpful - such as after partying hard, after overindulging, or on a difficult situation such as the death of a loved one*, or if you feel you've lost track in any sense or need a quick reset.

*It actually made it easier to be completely present and process everything at once with a certain degree of grace, as well as holding space for the others, rather than stuffing my face with food to numb down the sadness and other emotions (which everyone else was doing). I'd make a comparison to paying for something in cash as opposed to in several installments - sometimes you can afford to, and sometimes you can't.

The bold ones may choose to fast specifically on celebrations and holidays in order to break cycles, although in my experience, it's usually easier to either remove oneself from the situation or to compromise to an extent - it depends on where you are on your journey. It felt very weird to participate in birthdays, christmas and new years parties with 2-3 litres of either coconut water or juice. While I don't regret it, I felt so out of place, and disconnected to everyone else in there, that I might as well have missed it altogether and just stayed home... Although once I went on a day-long beach trip with a cooler and a few litres of watermelon juice... Not only was it extremely refreshing, but my skin got complimented by a dermatologist that was present (I was only 9 days into a juice fast at the time, and had had *severe* acne as a teenager).

Another idea would be following the stars - you could begin fasting on days of relevant alignments in the sky or specific transits in your natal chart. I personally enjoy fasting for one to three days every new moon, and sometimes full moons as well, and also during whole eclipse seasons. The equinoxes and solstices are also a wonderful time to fast on the day itself or for up to a week (or more) around it, to assist with clearing the old and stepping fresh into the new season.

So, for instance, one could choose to fast for one day every week, one to three days every new moon and/or one to seven days every change of seasons. Then, pick a time during spring and/or autumn to do a longer fast and really cleanse the house, at least once a year.

If you can and want to lose yourself in the woods, or have access to a farm or any place in the countryside, by all means, go. We absorb a lot from our environment, so trading the noise, stress and pollution from the city to the silence, peace and freshness of nature will greatly help you in going deeper within yourself, enhancing the detoxification process, and also avoiding common pitfalls such as the smell of your neighbours and restaurants' cooking food.

But ultimately, you will always fast where you are - here, and many of us may not have the opportunity to escape from the concrete jungle. Even if one was to flee to Eden, they would still have to carry all of their physical, mental, emotional and spiritual baggage to be sorted out regardless. We evolve not by running from our problems and circumstances, but by paying attention to and embracing them.

So again, immersion in nature would be a bonus, not a necessity. A vacation would be a bonus, not a necessity. A group of friends to support you would be a bonus, not a necessity. An ideal scenario, star alignment, place or conditions don't really exist - just take what you have available and make the most of it. But hey, if you've been blessed by a good hand of cards, it would be most foolish to not make good use of it. There is absolutely no need to make your life difficult on purpose.

Regardless of where you find yourself, it is an opportunity for self-growth and learning to create opportunities rather than relying on circumstances. Inner peace does not depend on what's happening around us, otherwise it would be called conditional peace.

8. HOW

Well, in actuality we are always fasting... Except when we're eating, which most people do a few times a day. So maybe I should change the title of this book to A Little Book on the Subtle Art of Disengaging our Eating Habits for Either Short or Long Periods of Time... but that would be too long!

In truth, there is absolutely nothing that has to be done. Each and every one of our cells contains the infinite wisdom of the whole universe. We grow up from an embryo spontaneously, just as our endocrine system and organs function by themselves, and cuts and bruises also heal by themselves. Our body is continuously and eternally doing its best to keep us alive, and all we have to do is allow it to do so. In fact, we do not die unless we are somehow unable to breathe. As we stop getting in the way of the body, it naturally knows what to do and will allocate its resources accordingly in order to heal us to an optimal state of health. The closer we get to this state, the less confused we become, as the more in tune we are with our own nature and personal needs.

To answer the how question in a more practical way: gently, deliberately, slowly, patiently and unpretentiously. In fact, the previous sections already present a comprehensible approach of how one can move from no experience towards shorter and then longer fasts. So rather than how to fast, I suppose it would make more sense to address how one would go about *starting* a fast.

Some people are way too conservative, others are way too daring. Some people might take months or even years to make use of this information and start to practice it, while others might order a juicer today and cold-turkey begin a 90 day juice fast next week. Either way can work, and either way can also not work. Just as I recommended each of us to find (or create) our own reason to fast, ultimately, we also have to get a feel for which speed we are most comfortable with cleansing, which will always vary depending on our current state of living and affairs. Remember though, hesitation is reverse hurry, and both will take you away from being in alignment with the universal rhythm. The music is already playing, you just have to figure out *if* you want to dance, and *how* you want to dance. What other people have done, are doing or will do is absolutely irrelevant… just pay a little attention so as to not bump into them!

"Nature never hurries, yet everything is accom-

plished."

"The journey of a thousand miles begins with a single step."

-   *Lao Tzu*

Keeping in mind that true healing is not just a long road, but a years, if not life-long endeavor, I tend to favor the gentle and slow approach, often taking baby steps, so long as they are consistent. You can't expect to finish an ultra-marathon by beginning with a sprint, especially if you've been out of shape. However, the beauty of this process is how we are constantly adapting and improving along the way, so that different methods can always be experimented, and since it isn't an actual race, you won't forfeit anything by stopping and resting every once in a while. In fact, I believe we all should find that balance between neither being lazy nor overexerting ourselves. So long as you're not walking backwards, you've already made a huge shift compared to the rest of society.

Since it isn't a race, that means there is no finish line either - unless you create one for yourself. Just keep going until you find a place you're comfortable with being, and remain there for as long as you wish to. We must figure out on our own which are our goals, what we deem as healthy, and what we are willing to compromise, if anything, for the sake of blending with society or indulging in certain pleasures. Your answer cannot be either right nor wrong, it will simply determine your fate and experiences. Either way, remember that so long as you're still breathing, it is never too late to change.

Plans can be useful, but there is no way to tell whether or not they are reliable, since life has too many surprises. Preparation, on the other hand, will always be useful, regardless of what the future unfolds. Therefore I say that more important than planning your fasts is being prepared to fast, which many find out they are not, only after starting. Call back to figuring out our own personal why. We must never forget why we're doing what we're doing, and in which direction we are heading towards.

I highly recommend not making your fast public to others, especially family. An exception would be any friends or group of individuals that are also into fasting, and therefore will be supportive of you, or may even be fasting at the same time. The last thing you need is having to deal with other people's BS* (when you already have plenty of your own to eliminate!) and negative assumptions - that never come from their own personal experience anyway, but rather are a repetition of the "common sense" we all have been indoctrinated with since birth. Lay low, do your thing, and then surprise them with your results.

*stands for both bullshit & belief systems.

Another exception is in the case you are living with other people. It would be sensible to give them, in short notice, a heads up that you won't be eating for a few days. You don't have to tell them for how long, but it would be wise to explain your reasoning, or what you're attempting to achieve. If doing so becomes too stressful, with them either thinking you're trying to harm yourself or being unable to understand you, it's always an option to pull the spiritual or religious card, and say you're doing it to get closer to [God]. Then, simply say you've been feeling so amazing and *connected with the divine*, that you wish to continue for a bit longer, and that when it's truly time to end it, you will *receive a message, or a sign, to do so.* Even if people have different interpretations of these words, they will remain true.

People are likely to be either religiously inclined, or at least open minded enough about science (if not both) that they can be presented scientific papers on the benefits of intermittent and short term water fasting. Either way, in due time, they won't be able to help but notice the difference in your mood and a certain aura around you. If they *see* you are doing good, even if they think you are starving yourself, they won't bother you too much. And if you don't attempt to force your ideals on them, it is almost guaranteed that eventually they'll become interested in trying what you're doing as well, even if only on a minor scale.

Many of us live as ugly ducklings without realizing our true potential, and fasting is one of the many ways of tapping into and allowing it to unfold. I guarantee there will be plenty of people curious and asking you what you did to suddenly look so healthy, glowing, at peace, younger, cheerful, etc. And in the case there aren't, then it may be time to ditch the ducks you've been hanging around with and go find the place where you can actually be-long, with a tribe that sees and values your true worth and well-being.

Mom once showed concern for how "thin" I was, at the end of a 21 days juice fast a few years ago. After immediately picking her up and walking around with her in my arms for a while, until she eventually told me to stop and put her down, she never again bothered me. Especially after witnessing how I not only kept up with my yoga practice, but made considerable improvements not only in terms of flexibility, but also in my inversions and arm balances. Images may be worth a thousand words, but actions go even beyond. Ideals may be questionable, but results are absolute.

Muscles are mostly water, and protein doesn't build them - exercising and putting a demand on your body does. People are mostly swollen, and that inflammation is what disappears with fasting. Our body never gets rid of that which is useful *and* is being used on a regular basis.

One could make a comparison between fasting and exerting self-control to a sort of mental weightlifting. So you could either begin with several reps of lighter weights (fruit eating, juice feasting), or very few reps of heavier weights (water or dry fasting), and slowly build it up in whichever way you're inclined to.

Intermittent fasting and up to 72 hours don't really require much preparation, although it is always sensible to have lighter, hydrating, fiber rich meals on the days before. I maintain that, to the average person, the practice of intermittent fasting, that is, reducing one's daily eating window to 8 hours or less, is the best way to prepare for longer periods of fasting.

Otherwise, you can begin doing 24-72 hours water or juice fasts whenever deemed appropriate, the latter being much easier. In fact, if you did something like starting your fast in the afternoon, you may have eaten something before it, and then you're still able to have dinner on the following day, after completing the 24 hour window. This would be a good idea for beginners. Gradually do 1 day fasts more often, and then tackle 2 and 3 day ones... see how long you can [more or less] comfortably go; and eventually you'll make it to a week. The first 3 days are always the most challenging, so why not practice them over and over?

Every time you do a short fast, you may choose to remove something from your grocery list. In other words, rather than going through a long fast at once, you could couple short fasts with making healthier choices in between them. This practice will allow one to start getting in touch with how it feels to be lighter in general, both in the mind and in the body, and how our energy levels differ based on what we consumed on the previous day.

When planning on doing a fast for longer than a week, it may be worth looking ahead and having an overall plan, such as knowing when, from where and how you'll be getting your groceries, if there would be any appointments or celebrations in that period, if you'll do all of your juices in the morning, or through the day as you consume them, etc. Although, in the end, these things will mostly be figured out on the go. The main difference from shorter fasts is that you know your whole lifestyle is bound to change for a longer period of time, so it involves a certain degree of commitment. Just like spending a month somewhere, as opposed to travelling only for the weekend. It is awkward at first, then eventually you get used to it, and in the end you often don't even feel like coming back home.

The more we try to control things, the more likely we are to trip on our own feet. I find it best to take each day at a time, and flow with our own rhythms; making peace with the mystery ahead, and learning to trust it. Dropping the expectations of what should and shouldn't happen, accepting that ultimately there are no certainties in life, and simply responding naturally to whatever arises in each day. Fasting is an act of faith - if not in [God], at the very least in the intelligence of our own bodies.

9. WHILE

"Sooner or later you're going to realize, just as I did, that there's a difference between knowing the path, and walking the path."
- *Morpheus*

Books, watching videos and reading about other people's experiences can only take us so far. Ultimately we have to take the leap of faith, endure the initial discomfort, and surrender to see where it will lead us. Change is often frightening or unpleasant at first, and other than moving up that scale of densities one step at a time, there isn't much we can do to avoid it. Once the previous trend has been broken, it begins to gradually get easier. Remember the cave analogy: at first, the fire burns our eyes. Then we get used to it, but the brightness from outside hurts our eyes once again. Then we get used to it, but the direct exposure to sunlight hurts us yet again. Only after overcoming all of these stages are we able to look at the sun and rejoice in all its benefits.

After one conquers the first three days,

and especially upon reaching a week, we can say a short fast has been successful, and many will choose to call it at this point. To the adventurous, determined, or more experienced ones, a medium or long fast has only begun. Now your body has officially adapted to what's going on; you've started to build a new momentum, and you've expelled most of the recent waste from your intestines. But even after a week of not eating, somehow there's still plenty yet to come out...

From there on, prepare to be amazed at the weird stuff that *will* be coming out. It may sound unpleasant, and it's not necessary to actually examine it, but I truly encourage getting acquainted with your wastes, after all, they are a result of the lifestyle you've been leading. If they are repugnant, what does it tell you? Seeing what comes out gives us a general idea of our inner state. Potential parasites aside, there will be all sorts of different shapes, textures, densities, smells and colours, which are an indicative of how long they've been *sticking* around.

There have been days where I only had one, or even no, bowel movements. On others, I'd have 3, or even up to 5, and sometimes more. I've actually clogged my toilet, more than once, upon eliminating not only high volume, but super sticky and dense sludge. After some point they will be mostly liquid-ish, almost like mud, but even several weeks into a fast I've eliminated plenty of small, very hard and weirdly shaped things. Some were very dry and had patterns engraved on them, literally looking like the shape of the intestines; almost puzzle pieces that had been lodged in there for years. Sometimes whatever came out was just so *weird*, and often covered in mucus, that I didn't think once before flushing it away instead of analyzing it. Plenty of stuff, in particular parasites, kinda gave away an "evil" or unpleasant aura of sorts. Yep, it is quite literally a shit show; sometimes even an exorcism. And this is just a heads up from someone who's currently 26... Keep in mind that even though I was quite curious and daring, over half of it was flushed away without being inspected. For the mad scientists out there, I'll recommend keeping a bucket, rubber gloves and wood skewers at hand.

If you can stomach it and are interested, you may research mucoid plaque for more details on this foreign matter that's inside most of us. Seeing what continues to come out is a most motivating experience, especially given how much better we feel after each elimination. To no longer be carrying around a bag of dried shit everywhere you go is worth celebrating!

For the brave and curious ones out there, I took a few pictures of what came out of me during late 2019 and 2020. I warn you that they are truly dirty and nasty images though. Proceed at your own risk. https://drive.google.com/drive/folders/1W-pVwonmGno0fELhVbscwuElbY5X-rsBo

On a side note, beware of not developing expectations of what should and should not come out of you, nor in which week it's supposed to happen. Just know what *something* will, and don't waste too much time analyzing or comparing it to what's coming out of other people. We each have our own unique shit to deal with.

If you're new to this sort of experience, re-member to *never* trust your farts during a juice cleanse, especially at the beginning of it. Also properly "chew" your juices, thoroughly mixing them with saliva, and avoid drinking them too fast. I also recommend to always have a plan B or enough ingredients for a second day of juicing, in case the fruit you bought wasn't good or fully ripe. Many also consider finishing eating what they had in the fridge and the pantry, or at least the most tempting stuff, before starting their fast. I call it a combination of the last supper with preemptive measures to avoid a disaster during a challenging moment later on.

How uncomfortable we find fasting for the first three days is a very accurate indicator of how unhealthy our lifestyle has been, as well as the degree of toxicity in the body. Most likely we have been in pain all along, but the daily food consumption kept numbing down our senses and overloading the nervous system. For reference, think of how a smoker is oblivious (numb) to the damage they're causing, but how obvious it is for everyone else around them. Now apply it to poor food choices (your smoker self) and fasting (yourself in recovery).

How weak and tired we feel shows how much we've been using food as a stimulant, and how much the body desperately needs to clean the house. How nervous, anxious, depressed, angry or restless we get shows just how much we are addicted to food and relying on it as an emotional crutch, or as a form of escapism from our daily lives and thoughts. How bored we get shows how much we've been using food as an entertainment to distract us from the present moment.

If the misery or feeling of discomfort is accompanied by many emotional ups and downs, as well as overall confusion, and gas, it's likely that some of our parasites are dying. With them, one can expect to also shed some of our false personas, identities and beliefs. Some aspects of us, or the ego, are likely to not make it out alive... But remember that we can only shed that which *has never been us* in the first place. Whatever survives the purge is our true self - or at least closer to it.

The longer we fast, the more we are relieved from afflictions we weren't even aware we had. But before those are eliminated, they must resurface, which forces us to revisit their pain, now in a more conscious state. Most people decide to quit here and bury these again, rather than enduring the temporary inconvenience and getting rid of them for good. Basically, we have to consciously undo all of the damage that we've done unconsciously. Afterwards, we become literally lighter, as we are carrying less deadweight both physically, mentally and emotionally. The relief that comes from releasing something that's been holding us back is a priceless feeling, and that will be experienced several times over the course of our healing journey.

Two very important things to do while fasting: remembering to relax, both mentally, emotionally, and physically. We often get worked up upon hearing something or contemplating certain thoughts, and that often translates into areas of our body being tensed up. The more we relax, the more we allow things to flow through us rather than stagnate. The other one is making sure we are supporting our organs of elimination. Most of the time we feel miserable during a fast is due to toxins (and associated emotions) being put into circulation in order to be purged, or the elimination of something that is taking too long to happen. It is very important to have at least one bowel movement everyday, and ways of assisting the body will be further elaborated in the Tools section.

Other than the movements through the backdoor, it is common to be coughing and sneezing mucus, to sometimes have pimples or rashes on our skin, and even an increase of mucus coming out of our eyes while we're asleep. Basically all orifices will be eligible to be used by the body in order to expel waste, and it will come through whatever's the path of least resistance.

Temporary headaches, nausea and other common "alarm system" symptoms are also normal. Remember they are a warning that there is waste disrupting our internal balance - in this case, it's been there all along, but simply went back into circulation in order to be eliminated. Usually having a bowel movement or taking a nap fixes it. Be mindful of not getting up too quickly as well, especially when water fasting, as we can get a bit lightheaded at times. Consider seeking help or breaking the fast if these states are too intense or take too long to go away.

But rather than being annoyed by these symptoms, do your best to embrace them as part of the process. Be fully present and get rid of them properly, and once will be enough. You can either think of it as an inconvenience, or be grateful that whatever's being purged will no longer be inside of you. Stress only happens when we resist. Dropping your expectations and training your adaptability is one of the best pieces of advice I can offer, both for fasting and also life in general.

Besides the garbage being removed and the parasites being evicted, all of the old and damaged cells must be gradually replaced by the new, healthy and superior version of ourselves. So it's very natural to have days of low energy, or needing to sleep a few hours more than we're used to. There will be days when we'll simply exist, and observe and bear with the elimination. Don't be fooled by appearances... The work-in during a fast is a non-stop process, and just like working out, it takes time for its results to manifest outwardly.

There will also be days when one will experience an abundance of energy, and even wake up earlier than usual, being fully rested, spontaneously. When exactly those shifts happen will be unique to each of us, and sometimes they are temporary, until the body begins detoxing deeper layers of tissue. They are a wonderful sign of progress, but don't be discouraged if you've been mostly tired. We all have different types of undoings to unwork upon.

I would compare fasting, or our healing journey and detox process in general, to a rollercoaster: there will always be ups and downs; sometimes you'll feel really low, while on other moments, really high (sometimes, literally). The amusing aspect, however, is how the whole roller coaster is dislocated, or rises, as we get healthier.

In other words, as we progress, the lowest points are higher than the previous lows, and the higher points also get higher. The average state of being, as related to a feeling of peace, vitality and joy, gradually increases.

It also happens that the alternation between the peaks and the valleys becomes less dramatic and frequent, and you begin to deviate less and less often from a natural high - which only keeps increasing. That is not, however, to say that there won't ever be difficult or challenging moments again... sometimes, even after much healing has already taken place, we may dip into an unexpected low. It's all part of the process, and if such a thing had happened early on, we might not have been ready to deal with it. On other times however, we may experience such unique bliss and a feeling of love and interconnectedness with all that our whole perspective on life will shift.

Other signs that one may experience during a fast are temporary bad smells, which will gradually dissipate to the point where you'll feel clean, even after sweating and not taking a shower for periods of time. Remember that if we have bad odors, it's because there's filth within us. Never suppress those, but rather find the cause, and eliminate it from our insides. Once it's gone, we'll realize we have a natural smell which is not unpleasant at all, and at least to me, the very idea of using things such as deodorants and perfumes became completely absurd.

In my experience our skin goes through different cycles when fasting, where sometimes a few pimples may pop up, but overall every few days, or at least every week, it continues to reach new degrees of softness and smoothness. It is a most satisfying feeling! Similarly, the mind will continue to get clearer and clearer with each passing day, as if a fog has been lifted. I relate both to the state of our intestines: the cleaner they are, the clearer will be both our mind and skin.

Our eyes are also a good mirror of what's going on inside, and although iridology is outside of my expertise, there will be a few references later on. However, anyone may pay attention to their sclera: the redness relates to the inflammation and acidity in our bodies, or how dis-eased we currently are. The less of it, or rather, the whiter it is, the more we are at ease.

The tongue is another wonderful indicator of our inner state. Simply put, a pink tongue is a sign of good health, while having a white layer on it is a sign of how much mucus we have covering (suffocating) our organs and cells. As we go deeper into a fast, the more we see this coating being formed, as things are surfacing in order to be eliminated. In some cases it can become quite thick and slightly colored, just like the different types of phlegm one coughs and sneezes away.

Some claim that when our tongue turns fully pink and clean again, we would have finished detoxing. Usually this layer also disappears, or at least is vastly reduced, when one breaks the fast, just like most "detox symptoms" are dissipated - which may give one a false impression of health being restored through eating. This would be like sweeping the dust under the carpet rather than throwing it away.

Relaxing is important enough to be re-emphasized a few times. Proper energy management is crucial during a fast, and most people don't realize how often they deplete themselves through emotional outbursts, overthinking, and keeping areas of the body tensed up. We should do our best to avoid stress and rest as much as it is convenient. For males, at least during a fast, semen retention is a must. For the couples, another recommendation will be looking into tantra, if you are not already practicing it. The seed has enough power to fertilize and bring forth a new life... use it responsibly, otherwise you'll be considerably sabotaging your health and longevity. Mantak Chia has good books about it, for both males and females.

Since we touched on the subject, any couple would do well to cleanse and purify their bodies *before* conception. However, no woman should begin a detoxification program when already pregnant or while breastfeeding. Do it before, or wait until afterwards. And please be mindful of what you allow the little ones to consume.

Shifting our attention backwards, avoid falling into the trap of blaming our parents for our current problems, because [most of the time] they did what they knew best, or at least what they could. Don't worry about what's already been done, and never attempt to hurry your detox process. Forgiveness, both towards others but also ourselves, is a wonderful catalyst for true healing, while blame only reinforces pre-existing patterns. Simply do your best with your current situation, and move from there at your own pace.

The more we fast, the more we become sensitive to different forms of energy and stimuli. This can be both a blessing and a curse, as with anything else... You will be more connected with your intuition, the subtle influences of being around different people and environments, as well as what you "consume" through your different sensory organs. Everything we are exposed to must be processed in some way, and may leave residues or some sort of impression behind if we're not careful.

So remove yourself from stressful situations without second thought, and also dismiss hanging out with people or watching anything that will negatively affect your mood. They say misery loves company, which is just another reason to learn how to be comfortable on your own. It also pays off tremendously to not watch the news, and overall filter which types of information and media we consume, such as music, conversations, books, videos, tv shows, people you follow on social media and so on. There's a reason why it's called *paying* attention - it is the most valuable currency, and determines what we're directing our energy to.

Another quality that is necessary for healing, or actually to achieve the most rewarding experiences in life, is patience. We all have had the experience of sending the car to the mechanic, or any other utensil, furniture or electrodomestic to maintenance. The common trend is that you can't use it until the repair has been over. Not so different with our bodies during a fast. Although it's not as if we were actually hibernating; it's just that its abilities and functionality will be temporarily restricted, as most of the energy and resources are being redirected to the healing process.

To invoke the words of the Tao Te Ching yet again: there is a time for being ahead, and a time for being behind. A time for being in motion, and a time for being at rest. A time for being vigorous, and a time for being exhausted. Rather than struggle, simply honor where you are.

"Refine your senses a little more each day. Eventually, your awareness will pierce deeply into your body and into the world. Then you'll think less and feel more,

enjoying even the simplest things in life, and no longer addicted to achievement or expensive entertainment."
- *Dan Millman*

Juice feasting is a most wonderful way to cleanse the accumulated filth and start digging... but keep in mind that exploring distilled water and dry fasting is what will really uncover and renew the darkest depths of themselves - if you feel called and inclined to do so.

Similar to rabbit holes, we find that the deeper we venture into ourselves, the deeper it is. Physical, mental, emotional and spiritual transformation go hand in hand. The deeper we dig, the more we'll immerse ourselves in the shadows of our subconscious, and the biggest will be the potential for transformation. Remember that seeds grow in the dark... so if you find yourself lost in the darkness, rather than falling into despair, start sowing! Instead of attempting to use your physical eyes [which may be unable to see a thing], train to go beyond the five senses, and develop your inner vision. Not everyone is interested in this kind of process, just like many remain in the shallow waters when going to the beach. That's not a sign of weakness, just a personal choice, so never force yourself into something you don't want or feel ready to. Although it is said that the things we are afraid of doing are exactly what we should do in order to grow...

Just like the sun rises and falls everyday, and we observe different seasons of both planetary and universal scales, the same process also takes place in the individual. Similar to a phoenix, or a snake, only through the shedding of our past selves, which then becomes fertilizer, can we allow the formation of the new. Nothing in existence is either created or destroyed: only transformed and rearranged. Life and death depend on each other, and this is also represented by the butterfly. During a fast, we're essentially inside of a cocoon, where our cells are cleansing and transforming themselves to give birth to our new avatar. We must be patient and bear with the process if we wish to spread our wings afterwards. If you want to be reborn, then let yourself die.

"Opportunities to find deeper powers within ourselves come when life seems most challenging."
-   *Joseph Campbell*

10. TRIPPING

I know what you're thinking... and in fact, my first time doing a heroic dose of psilocybin was during a coconut water fast and an eclipse - and what an amazing, magical experience that was. However, to anyone planning on taking mind-altering substances during a fast, remember how you'll be extra-sensitive, more open and vulnerable, which means the experience may be deeper and more rewarding than you ever imagined, but also much more intense than you signed up for. Be responsible.

This section is actually to remind us that fasting is not about perfection, but about loving (or remembering how to love) every inch of ourselves, and (re)aligning with our truest nature, which involves patience, respect and sincerity.

Many were the times I broke a fast with cooked foods, or splurged big time for days in a row right after a fast, or quit earlier than I wanted to, gave in to temptation for all sorts of different reasons, decided to "just have a bite" and end up having a whole meal, tried something as an experiment and fell back into old habits for not only days, but sometimes weeks or even months, and a few other similar missteps.

None of those were mistakes though, but lessons. And quite a few I've had to take over and over, until I finally realized that temptation is the best advice of what NOT to do. It is perfect (reverse) guidance. And after the lesson has been learned, it all boils down to willpower and perseverance. May you learn from my experiences! If not, then be gentle with yourself as you go through your own rollercoaster.

Sometimes it's all about enduring a bit longer, but it's also necessary to be sensible enough to realize when to step back and re-stabilize yourself, rather than recklessly pushing forward non stop or in a hurry. Otherwise one is more likely to trip on their own feet, and fall either straight on their face or even backwards, and "lose some ground", so to speak. Fasting is the *fastest* way to health, but *it is not a race*. It must be treated as a marathon, or rather as a long distance hike, and not as a sprint...

Steady progress matters more than your actual speed. Simply keep track of your goal as to avoid going sideways (too often). Every journey will be perfectly imperfect, just as we are. It is not about being hard on yourself either, or you'd risk either breaking apart or sacrificing experiences that you may come to regret later on. That is, avoid becoming obsessed with cleansing to the degree you'd be pushing yourself too fast and not honoring your personal needs.

We must be firm, but also gentle, and just like water, adapt to each day's situations. Another way of putting it would be as a dance, where our mind is the active partner, and the body, the passive. It is not about controlling our body through force and austerity, otherwise even if results are accomplished, it would eventually rebel. The reverse is more common, as we see that most people's minds are slaves to their bodily demands, and we also know how this ends. The relationship we are aiming for is not that of a master and a servant, but of lovers. Just like in a dance, we should aim for the mind to simply lead the way, in a gentle and respectful, but also decisive manner.

The soft overcomes the hard not through force, but by the means of persistence. And that's exactly what we are doing when only drinking liquids: we use the water to dissolve and wash away all of our accumulated impurities and blockages. As that happens on a physical level, changes also take place simultaneously on the emotional, mental and spiritual planes.

Although miraculous things can happen upon fasting for 40+ days in a row, completely cleansing the body is a task that is likely to take a few years. We're undoing not only decades, but generations of addictive behavior... that started from even before we were born! So more important than simply pushing ourselves is changing our mindset and beliefs. Once we do, it is only a matter of time until our actions and habits adjust on their own.

We should aim to see either a monthly or seasonal net gain, with minor but consistent improvements. It is better to take 3 steps forward followed by 2 backwards than to not move at all. We all have difficult moments and situations to face, and our stock of willpower can't be full all of the time. It is crucial to learn how to pick our battles, as well as accepting to yield some of them in order to win the war.

The small changes all. Imagine how a simple 1° difference would completely change the destination a ship or airplane would arrive in. Alternatively, if we were to compound 1% everyday, at the end of one year we would have either (1.01) ^ 365 = 37.80, or (0.99) ^ 365 = 0.03. Meanwhile, (1.00) ^ 365 always remains 1.00.

In other words, by the end of a year stacking 1% of daily progress, one will achieve 37 times what they had at first. Yes, it is actually 3680% more, and not just 365%... it's the beauty of the compound effect. Or, by doing 1% less everyday, one would end with 33 times less, or only 3% of what they used to have or be. By not changing any-thing, what a surprise, nothing changes.

"We are what we repeatedly do. Excellence, then, is not an act, but a habit."
- *Will Durant*

Fasting is a time for revision, not suffering. Stress happens when we resist, so the key is al-lowing the detox to happen, while being present for it. It may not always feel pleasant at the time, but it will afterwards. If we want something we never had, we must be willing to do something we never did... If we simply stop eating but refuse to address our traumas or reflect on our own lives and rearrange our priorities, we are likely to sim-ply gravitate back towards our previous lifestyle eventually.

That happens because much more often than they'd like to admit, people are eating to deal with or suppress their emotions, or out of addic-tion and habit, and not out of hunger. You know, there is a reason gluttony is one of the seven *deadly* sins. Just as lack of something can be a problem, anything superfluous or in excess is also offensive. The answer always lies in balance and harmony.

We've seen how the food residues and in-organic material that accumulates inside of our bodies result in water retention in order to iso-late them. If we were to associate our mind and thoughts with the air element, then our feelings could be represented by water. Emotions can be seen as energy-in-motion, so with that we have physical constipation resulting in emotional constipation, as that water stagnates in regions of our body. It represents our different traumas and feelings that have been buried inside of us (usually through consuming food, drugs, or simply denial), and also weigh us down and condition our behavior to a certain degree. Once we start purging, those will gradually come to the surface in order to be processed and eliminated, which means we have no choice but to address them if we wish to move forward.

Suppressing things will never work in the long term - how long can you keep a beach ball underwater? It is necessary to fully express them, without reservations, and then let them go. Energy in motion is never a problem, but when it stagnates, it becomes a blockage. Whatever we resist, persists. Instead of struggling, we must embrace, and then redirect, overwrite, dissolve or transcend it. Dealing with our traumas is much easier by pulling a sort of emotional aikido than by attempting to strike them down with force.

The key lies in how to allow those stagnated feelings to be expressed in a constructive or cathartic way. We all know if we're not careful, it's easy to discharge them onto other people who have nothing to do with it. Much better would be to do so through exercising, or playing a musical instrument, writing in a journal, talking to someone, etc. Skills, or disciplines, are essentially ways of self-expression. Find whatever works for you and start practicing it on a daily basis, even if you don't intend to share it with others.

As we have physical constipation (shit) that leads to emotional constipation (repressed feelings), we also end up with a case of mental constipation (rooted beliefs and a foggy or confused mind). They are simply different densities of stagnated energy. Most people only attempt to solve one of these issues, without being aware of how they're all interconnected, which is why they often fail to succeed.

The more we purge, the less dense we become. The less dense we are, the easier it is to vibrate in higher frequencies. States of being (electromagnetic fields) such as anger, sadness, jealousy, worry, doubt, fear are all low in vibration and result in contraction. Others such as joy, serenity, enthusiasm, love and gratitude are way up in the scale, and promote expansion and harmony. That doesn't mean we won't experience the latter unless we completely cleanse our insides, it's just that it becomes easier to reside in them as our natural state.

The emotions that arise when we're detoxing can also serve as a clue to which organ is being cleansed, or has been most damaged. According to traditional chinese medicine, different emotions are stored in different organs. For example, anger is related to the liver, fear with the kidneys, joy with the heart, sadness and grief with the lungs, and worry with the spleen. Then you have a wide range of ways of going about it, many being mentioned in the Tools section.

There is also the case of unconsciously absorbing emotions from our environment, such as from watching tv, listening to music or being in stressful places, especially while eating, which means they end up somewhat attached to the food that is ingested, and processed alongside it. Remember that all the vibrations we expose ourselves to can be treated as food.

It is important to pay attention to what triggers specific thoughts and feelings through the day, and how we often seek food to distract ourselves from those, that is, muffling them, as opposed to being present and seeing where they stem from. Could be due something that happened last week, or maybe something repressed from your childhood. Investigate, unbury, process, then release (express).

At each moment, we are either making excuses in order to re-cycle patterns, which only increases their power, or we make the choice to break their momentum and create a new rhythm to replace it. In the latter case, we must remember that it takes time to re-adjust, and for the new pattern to gain momentum and become natural. We just need to continue "winning" these moments, little by little. If we don't have self control, then something, or someone else, does. Are you playing the game of life, or are you being played?

"As a single footstep will not make a path on the earth, so a single thought will not make a pathway in the mind. To make a deep physical path, we walk again and again. To make a deep mental path, we must think over and over the kind of thoughts we wish to dominate our lives."

- *Henry David Thoreau*

Remember that we have no opponents but ourselves. Blaming other people or circumstances won't get us anywhere, regardless of what it is. There is no one controlling us, but there is a lot of manipulation and misdirection going on, just like in a magic act. Ultimately the issue is not something forced onto us, but rather our unconscious (re)action of accepting a suggestion to sabotage our own selves.

Forgiveness is not about "them", it is about you, and releasing that burden of holding on to whatever happened. You may take as much time as necessary to process whatever event happened, but eventually you'll have to make a choice of whether you have become wounded by it (crippled), or wiser as a result of it (stronger). Whether you've found an obstacle that stunts your growth, or a stepping stone that will allow you to climb even higher than you ever thought possible, is up to your own perspective and attitude.

Fasting is much more of a mental and emotional challenge than a physical one. First you have an illusion of feeling weak, while the truth is your body is performing an amazing process of healing inside, that requires a lot of energy. Then, there's a simple reason people feel good again when they break a fast: the body halts the detox process in order to deal with the food. Again why understanding what's happening underneath and having a reason for going through is so important. They are the compass that will prevent us from getting lost in the journey.

Most people are only looking for excuses to continue to sabotage themselves, as they are too afraid of putting in the work to reclaim their freedom and sovereignty. After all, that would require leaving their comfort zones. So instead, they sacrifice long-term, long-lasting health, peace and joy for the sake of short-term, fleeting pleasures. Remember the cave... it is easier to keep looking at the shadows than getting up and facing the light. It is but an illusion, as one would only further cripple themselves in continuing doing so.

"Whatever deceives men seems to produce a magical enchantment."

- *Plato*

A drug is defined as any substance that has a physiological effect when ingested or introduced into the body, that is to say, alters the functions of the body to a certain degree either physically and/or psychologically. Opioids, in particular morphine, are known for their analgesic properties, that is, their ability to suppress pain by altering our sensitivity through interfering with our nervous system.

Exorphins are opioids derived from the digestion of protein from either animal or plant sources (I have not found whether all fruits and vegetables have them, as most studies seem to focus on wheat and dairy - which are the ones with a higher concentration of those, and also widely known as comfort foods...). Overall they seem to be present in animal products and grains in particular. It is worth researching this topic if you're interested in becoming aware of just how much we're eating out of addiction rather than necessity.

Emotional eating is the main cause of diseased bodies and prolonged suffering, as excess food only suppresses the pain and makes us numb to it rather than addressing its cause. If what's coming out is waste... then just how much did we have to eat to begin with?

The more we eat foods high in exorphins,

the more we condition our nervous system to rely on those to relieve pain and stress, and that may even decline the production of endorphins by our own body. It is no wonder we end with a case of dependency, as we observe common withdrawal symptoms from drugs when we begin a fast, or improve our food choices in general. Those may include mood swings, sweating, tearing eyes, muscle aches, vomiting, nausea, hot and cold flushes, increased heart rate, poor concentration and memory, restlessness, irritability, depression, and a few others... Essentially, detox symptoms from the body eliminating whatever residues of these substances were left inside of us, and a recalibration of our nervous and endocrine system.

This is another reason why I recommend playing with intermittent fasting and short fasts before jumping on longer ones - it is not a joke or exaggeration to say that we have been addicted to all sorts of foods. Drugs provide an illusion of comfort through sedation. When we begin to fast, we become aware of the pain that has been suppressed for decades. The good news is that those symptoms greatly subside after a few days, or at most a few weeks.

As we cleanse ourselves and our body begins to properly produce endorphins again, we begin to feel those high vibrational feelings without having to rely on external substances. We (re)learn how to feel good and happy without crutches or conditions, that is, how to generate bliss internally as opposed to depending on temporary euphoria triggered by external sources. It is essentially a reclamation of sovereignty.

"We shall avoid pain, always, and seek for pleasure. But of pleasures there are two kinds: for the first, and false, pleasures, we must pay too high a price: the sacrifice of our physical health and peace of mind. And without our health and peace of mind we are unable to enjoy any pleasures. The second kind of pleasures are our eternal companions - these noble pleasures are the enjoyment of all beautiful things in Nature: the mountains, the forests, the oceans, the colors of the sunrise and sunset... all that is beautiful in man's creation: great books, great music, great works of art, friendship and love... The wise shall have as their program of living, the gradual replacement of the false pleasures with our eternal companions, the noble pleasures of life."

- *Epicurus*

It's infinitely better to be in recovery than in denial. The first implies awareness of the problem and a desire for change; while the latter, a weak, lazy, or ignorant mind.

Again, it is not about punishing ourselves, but simply making more intelligent choices. Short-term pleasures often result in long-lasting problems and dependency, while some degree of discipline and self-control create a foundation for long-lasting health, vitality and happiness. The best things in life remain free... So find your own balance.

It is also useful to learn how to focus on solutions rather than on problems. Once you identify your main triggers, be it people, a time of the day or social circumstances, you can begin to prepare counter-measures to prevent yourself from falling in those pitfalls, which could easily lead you towards repeating pre-conditioned cycles of behavior.

Something that is almost guaranteed to put you back in control: fully exhale and then take a few slow, deep breaths. Some light stretching and a glass of warm water also helps, or simply continue with the breathing for 5 to 15 minutes. After re-centering yourself, you'll be able to look at the situation objectively and decide whether or not you truly want to indulge. The warm water is due the fact we're often dehydrated more than anything else, and it tends to be enough to satiate us.

The more we add things, the more we disrupt our homeostasis, which is why consuming something often leads us into a snowball effect of splurging. This is particularly true in the case of dehydrating substances, such large amounts of sodium chloride. Most often It's not food that we want... it's water. On a positive perspective, due to our increased sensitivity, we often feel the harmful effects of becoming heavy, bloated or thirsty much easier and quicker, which helps contrast the different densities of being. The more we feel the pain, the less we'll want to hurt ourselves.

Remember that temptation isn't a problem; only lack of self-control, is. It is not the circumstances that ultimately determine who we are, but our choices. However, if you can't handle your current surroundings, then temporarily change them. Self-control is a skill, and as any other skill, only by constant practice will we get better at it.

"Our greatest glory is not in never failing, but in rising up every time we fail."
-      *Ralph Waldo Emerson*

11. TOOLS

Although our bodies do everything on their own when we get out of the way, mastering the art of applying the right leverage, in the right place, at the right time, can provide immense assistance and considerably ease its duties.

It just so happens the best and most effective tools for healing and self-transformation tend to be free, simple, and always available. But remember to treat them as a convenience, and not a necessity. While it is wise to make use of anything we have at our disposition, it won't do good to become dependent on them. This whole section is optional, as the only thing you need before starting a fast is a strong commitment.

The most important advice I would give anyone is in regards to conscious deep breathing, which is also referred to as pranayama, breathwork or breathing exercises. If liquid fasting and enemas are purification through water, and dry fasting, sunshine and physical exercises purification through fire, then deep diaphragmatic breathing would be a purification through air (that in turn creates a bit of fire).

Most people are shallow breathers. The thing is, most of the blood vessels are concentrated in the lower part of our lungs, so it is literally inefficient to breathe in this way. Most of our metabolic waste, as well as a substantial part of the detox, happens through the purification of our blood in the lungs. Deep diaphragmatic breathing not only increases the efficiency of this process, but it also massages our internal organs and helps with peristalsis.

A way of starting would be to develop gentle, deep, rhythmic, silent, long breaths. Keep your spine straight and either kneel, sit cross legged on the floor, or on the edge of a chair. Half or full lotus have been my favorite positions. Breathe in and out through the nose, and keep your tongue on the roof of your mouth. Rest your hands on your thighs, knees, or perform any mudra of your preference. Then, rather than paying attention to your nose, focus on the outwards-pushing and inwards-pulling movement of your diaphragm. That is, breath primarily with your belly, not with your chest. The flow of air in and out the lungs is a consequence of this motion, and not the cause. By focusing on the wave-like movement of our diaphragm, the breath naturally becomes deeper, rhythmic, silent and longer on its own.

If you get distracted, attempt to return your attention to your abdominal region. Alternatively, you can simply follow the flow of air going inside and outside of your lungs, or observe any other aspect or region of your insides. As your breathing slows down to 3 or less breaths per minute and your sessions go beyond 15 minutes in stillness, you'll enter a whole new realm. If you reach the point of sustaining 1 minute breaths comfortably for 40 minutes and longer, you'll begin to have experiences that can't quite be expressed in human words. The more you practice conscious deep breathing or different breathing exercises on a daily basis, the easier and more natural fasting will feel like - remember our pyramid of needs.

The effort required to move your diaphragm is an indicator of how much the intestines are filled with residues and the internal organs, inflamed and swollen. Fully exhaling and pulling the navel towards the spine, creating a sort of vacuum, is a wonderful way of assessing the situation. When doing so, you can also use your hands to gently massage your intestines, which greatly helps to loosen up and move things.

The next one will be to sleep as much as you can and need. Overall, when tired, bored or confused, taking a nap is probably the best choice one can make during a fast - that is, if there is no willpower for a session of deep, conscious breathing. Especially at first, it is not a time to be on the move and break records, but to rest as much as it is convenient, so the body can heal itself. When you have the energy, use it... when you don't, don't. It's not rocket science. I would also avoid staying up late at all costs. Remember that maintenance is only temporary.

Also invest as much time in being exposed to the sun as possible. Heliotherapy is a thing. It is not only a way of cleansing the skin, but it also reaches and purifies the blood. In particular, many benefits come from exposing our private parts to it, although it is not necessary to do so. The sun is also a source of energy, if that wasn't obvious by now. Plants and machines make use of it, so why wouldn't we? The daring ones would do well to research the ancient art of sungazing.

That said, my "fasting starter pack" would most certainly include a water distiller, a citrus or slow masticating juicer, a neti pot, and an enema bag.

Make sure the distilled water machine chosen will attend to your family needs, the interior is made of stainless steel, and a good bonus would be having the recipient made of glass rather than plastic.

Not much to be said about juicers... If one wants to stick to orange and mandarin only, they could get by with even a cheap citrus juicer. For anything else, you can't even begin to compare fruit and vegetable juices freshly made from a slow masticating juicer to something store bought or improvised in a blender. Just pick one that fits your budget and is not too painful to clean.

A neti pot is incredibly useful for loosening up mucus and clearing the sinus area. I used it many times, in particular in the morning and before bed.

An enema bag is probably the best investment I made after the juicer and the water distiller. While it's not something one should rely on, at the risk of conditioning their bodies, it is a most wonderful tool - although a bit daring to approach at first. After the third time doing it or so, it became natural, and even if it feels weird at first, the release and relief that comes afterwards is well worth it. We've consumed the most abnormal, sticky, glue-like substances over the course of decades... it is only reasonable to help the body with its elimination. I highly recommend using it at the beginning of a fast, and whenever one goes by a day without a bowel movement, as well as whenever one feels miserable without apparent reason - it is often the body struggling to purge old, sticky stuff. The most common options to use are water, herbal teas, or coffee.

Orin, popularly referred to as urine, is a bit of a controversial topic. The majority of people consider it a waste (because they were taught so), while a minority of people consider it the elixir of youth (because they read books and experimented with it). The fact that documents from China, Egypt and India dated thousands of years back address the practice of consuming one's own orin should be enough to get anyone intrigued by it... But if it doesn't, just skip the next two paragraphs.

It is something that could be entirely dismissed or become a complete game-changer - but that depends on you. I'm not sure the body would eliminate waste through the same channels that give birth to life, after all. Among its benefits are the presence of hormones, stem cells, information about our bodies, and tons more. About 90% of it is simply distilled water from our blood, with any substances that were present in excess. Some claim it provides a sort of homeopathic effect, others claim it's just a placebo, and a few would go as far as saying it's a miraculous substance that can solve all of our problems. If it tastes or smells bad, or looks disgusting in any way, what does that tell you about the state of your own blood? Urea is present in most beauty lotions and creams, by the way. Why outsource it?

I've had on and off periods of playing with

it since 2018 or so. From my experience so far, I've noticed it to be amazing for our skin, and taken internally, to be a sort of elixir that simply boosts my overall energy and vitality, although nothing *too* amazing. It also helps loosening up and expelling mucus, as well as promoting digestive health. The first time I've expelled parasites was after doing aged orin enemas in late 2019. Now *that* was life changing, and since then I've often used part aged orin (4+ days), part hot water when I do enemas. The aged version is quite strong to drink, and seems to bring a whole other level of benefits, though I haven't explored it enough to discuss. It is definitely superior than fresh to be applied on the skin, and many agree on its potential to eliminate parasites. During that period I've eliminated dozens of 6-8 inches string-like parasites covered in mucus, with a few being around a foot, and the longest one more than half a meter. You can see some of them in the link from before.

Herbs can be very useful for supporting the organs of elimination, assisting with the repair of the endocrine system, or killing parasites. For this, one should really do their own research or find a reliable professional or brand that already sells pre-made formulas. Common ones would be the use of wormwood + black walnut hull capsules to kill parasites, burdock for the liver, dandelion for the kidneys, and cascara sagrada is a *very potent* intestinal cleanser.

Food grade diatomaceous earth is also, allegedly, a very effective parasite killer. I'm not quite sure how effective this one was in this regard, but I definitely feel it helped ease my cravings in general. I would usually take a teaspoon with warm water after a meal or in the morning, sometimes also mixed with apple cider vinegar and/or activated charcoal, for up to a few weeks at a time.

Psyllium husk, bentonite clay and activated charcoal is a somewhat famous combination to cleanse the intestinal tract. Robert Morse's "GI Broom" has a good reputation, although I never had the opportunity to use it. Arnold Ehret lists an interesting "intestinal broom" formula in his book, as a combination of a few things mentioned here and many others. I've witnessed good results from using it, but I've also had good results when not using it. There was a time when I was having fun exploring herbs in general, but now it's been a while since I've lost interest - follow your own intuition, not what others tell you to do. Just because it worked for some doesn't mean it will for you, and vice-versa.

Especially when juice fasting, it is important to pay a certain degree of attention to our oral hygiene. Whenever you've finished your juices and won't be drinking more in the next few hours, waiting about 30 minutes and then washing your mouth with water & baking soda is very helpful, as well as lightly brushing the teeth. Aside from baking soda, raw cacao powder, turmeric and activated charcoal can also be used as a substitute for conventional toothpaste, and there are many other diy recipes on the internet. One could also choose to do oil pulling in the morning and/or at night, as well as scraping their tongue.

Consulting with an iridologist or getting books, watching videos and attempting to figure the basics by oneself, can give us a reading of the overall situation of our body, the most damaged organs and glands, as well as our genetic predispositions. Dr Bernard Jensen's book is a good introduction to the subject.

It can be very useful to get yourself a foot and/or hand reflexology charts, as well as the traditional chinese medicine organ clock. This way, either through the iridology research or by seeing at what time of the day you feel different emotions, urges or discomfort, you can begin to map out patterns, triggers and their origins. Conscious deep breathing coupled with acupressure points in our hands or feet are a quick way to address those and return to a neutral, peaceful state.

As effective and rewarding pressure points may be, it also pays off to simply disregard them and massage the soles of our feet and the palms of our hands with our thumbs, in a spontaneous and intuitive manner. You'd basically be indirectly massaging all of your organs and glands, as well as developing some quality alone time and getting acquainted with your own body. Whenever you find a spot that feels particularly good or relaxing, play with it!

Going beyond our extremities, it is also wonderful to gently massage our whole bodies, either with our hands or through dry skin brushing. It doesn't matter if it's only a 3 minutes thing, or a whole hour session. Again another way of developing intimacy with ourselves, and also moving the lymphatic system and promoting relaxation. If you have a partner to exchange massages with, rejoice and make good use of it!

Whenever you have the energy, it is highly recommended to move your body in a way you find pleasant and enjoyable. It helps with circulation, maintaining your vitality and strength, and also with elimination. The most simple (although super effective) ways would be going for walks, using a rebounder, or stretching yourself. If you can, do at least some degree of movement on a daily basis.

My favorite ones are yoga and qigong, which I do every morning and sometimes at night. Qi-gong means breath or energy work, so it contemplates a vast array of practices. There are many different sets and styles, but it usually consists of either repeating a few exercises or maintaining a particular stance for a period of time (zhan zhuang). Taijiquan can be seen as a form of qigong, but it is really a chinese internal martial art that provides not only self defense but also health and spiritual benefits. It is more complex than most qigong sets, and requires a skilled instructor to learn.

Yoga is an indian system comprising 8 limbs, of which most people only know of the asanas and pranayama (3rd and 4th). Asanas are a series of physical postures with the purpose of conditioning the body for more advanced energy practices, while pranayama are breathing exercises to purify the body and discipline the mind. I'd say meditation is anything you do with absolute awareness and presence, though most people only relate it to sitting practices.

I can vouch for the book Light on Yoga by B. K. S. Iyengar, as well as The Eight Treasures taught by Glenn Hairston (or any other variation of the Baduanjin you like) and the Flying Phoenix system taught by Terence Dunn. Dynamic Strength by Harry Wong provides a wonderful set of warming up and isometric exercises.

Regardless of what you gravitate towards, I highly recommend at least 15 minutes of basic stretching daily. It is also worth learning from cats and animals in general, who often stretch gently through the day. You can also do the exhalling, navel towards the spine, vacuum exercise at any time.

For example, one could do a few rounds of sun salutations (or cat-cows), and then 15 to 90 seconds in each of the following asanas: malasana, parivrtta janu sirsasana, upavistha konasana, baddha konasana, paschimottanasana, gomukhasana, matsyendrasana, balasana, then 1 to 15 minutes in savasana (or even fall asleep, if done at night). Aside from those, I've seen great benefits in terms of releasing gas or assisting bowel movements through the practice of sirsasana, sarvangasana, halasana, and either sarpasana or salabhasana. An overall tip regarding yoga: if your breathing becomes heavy or irregular, you're probably pushing yourself too far.

Physical flexibility is also connected with emotional and mental adaptability. The more rigid and inflexible our bodies are, the more restricted we are in expressing our feelings and holding on to beliefs and outdated ways of thinking. Releasing blockages affects mobility in all levels.

Of course, on days you have been feeling more energetic, especially if you're going on juices, you're free and encouraged to engage in calisthenics or any other form of workout you enjoy, and I would also recommend dancing or swimming. Any type of core exercises, such as bicycle crunches, is a great way to assist with elimination. Just remember that until you've done a considerable amount of healing, it is best to do maintenance work rather than pushing your limits.

Singing is also a wonderful way of expressing yourself and doing some unconscious breathwork. Take any opportunity you can to laugh and smile, which provides an immediate uplifting of our mood.

Other than crying (when you feel compelled to), submerging ourselves in natural bodies of water such as waterfalls, lakes, rivers and the ocean, as well as showering in the rain, are wonderful ways of cleansing our soul and releasing stored emotions. Even taking a bath or visiting the sauna can provide considerable results.

Forest bathing, walking barefoot on the earth, grounding, hugging trees, smelling flowers and any other form of connecting with nature are great ways of reinvigorating ourselves and releasing stress. Not only trees though; but make sure to hug other humans and animals (who are willing to be hugged) as much as you can. Research the benefits from physical touch if you find this silly or unnecessary.

Although there's great value in literally retreating from the world during a fast, it can be quite daunting at times, so it is only wise to use technology in our favor. Being part of groups in social media or texting apps, forums, or simply being active in youtube channels that are focused on fasting and healing, can be a great tool to connect with others that are going through similar experiences, to both offer and receive a helping hand. I highly recommend finding at least one, or even a few people who are "walking their talk", and following their journey for inspiration and motivation. Both watching youtube videos and reading other books about fasting, as well as other people's stories, can be very helpful, and also keep us on track if things get rough. Chris Manly is one of the most inspiring people I've met in this regard, as well as Monica Schutt. They're both beautiful and sincere beings who've done a lot of inner work and healing, and now have been sharing their wisdom and experiences.

Something I dare say everyone should look into is learning about the etymology and true meaning of words, as well as paying attention to certain expressions and ways of speaking we've incorporated unconsciously. It is not called "spelling" for no reason - talking is literally spellcasting.

Whenever we affirm something, we are giving it our energy, whether we realize it or not. So never say something you don't wish to be true, and never identify yourself with limitations, be it beliefs, dis-ease names or conditions. Instead of saying you are sick, or unhealthy, poor, unlucky, incompetent, weak, addicted, or any other similar, say that you've only been acting in a certain way instead. Don't identify those states as who you are, but simply as a way you've behaved in the past - and no longer does in the present. Otherwise you're only reinforcing those ideas and qualities, instead of being open to change.

A good example would be to use investing, which means a return is being expected, instead of spending, which implies a wasteful action with no return. If you're not receiving it back, then your energy is being appropriated by someone else... Which of the two actions have you been doing with your time and attention?

Another pointer would be to focus on the "positive" rather than on the "negative". Instead of saying "I'm not poor", you'd rather say "I am rich". If you say the first, you're still emphasizing the "poor" aspect, even if indirectly. So instead of choosing to deny a perception of lack, focus on embodying a state of abundance.

Affirmations may seem like a silly thing at first, but do some research and play with practicing them daily for a week, and the results will speak for themselves. It can be a wonderful tool for changing our perception of ourselves and uplifting our mood, as well as clarifying how we envision the best, most successful, happy and healthy version of ourselves - so we can begin to embody it.

Keeping a gratitude journal to write on every morning and/or every night is a way of going about it instead of reciting them out loud, and you can also choose to listen to youtube videos that repeat affirmations you identify with on a loop; or even record an audio yourself. The key is saying "I am" and identifying yourself with those states right now, instead of saying "I will" or "someday". Don't create a distance between yourself and your desired state, because we always live in the now. If we're gonna use words to communicate, then we might as well use them to our own advantage.

Speaking of youtube videos, it is also amazingly helpful to listen to high vibrational instrumental music, such as those tuned to any of the solfeggio frequencies, binaural beats, or any other that suits your tastes. Research the difference between 432 and 440hz if you haven't already, and pay attention to how listening to different styles of music can immediately impact both your mood and mental state.

Listening to music, reciting affirmations, doing visualization exercises, watching tv, listening to the radio, complaining, worrying, daydreaming or praying are essentially the same activity. It's just a matter of choosing which types of seeds you're going to cultivate, as the subconscious mind nurtures whatever is planted in it without any concept of discrimination or judgment. It is up to the conscious mind to determine what is going to be harvested in the future.

I highly recommend starting your day with a few words (could be in silence) of gratitude, affirmations, or prayer, followed by at least a few minutes of deep diaphragmatic breathing, and also ending your days in a similar manner. I find it particularly powerful to do visualization at night, while already laying in bed. Imagine yourself healed and living the life of your dreams, in perfect health and bliss, in your ideal scenario, with your ideal company, and expressing the most amazing and fulfilled version of yourself that you can envision. Drop all resistance and uncertainty, forget the how, and simply fall asleep *feeling* that reality as your present state - not something you wish to happen, but something you are already experiencing and living. Then see how your life changes.

12. AFTER

Learning about fasting and its benefits, that is, acquiring the knowledge, could be compared to the hero receiving a call to adventure. Then applying the knowledge, or starting the fast, would be the moment the hero embarks on their journey, with the trials encountered being all of the detox symptoms and purging experienced. This chapter, or breaking the fast, relates to the hero returning home after finally slaying the monster and finishing the quest, which are represented by the purging of the filth and parasites that inhabited their intestines. The monster is not an external creature - it lies hidden within each of us.

After being reborn through trials and tribulations, the hero returns alive, but not as the same person they used to be. The journey resulted in personal growth, and they are now equipped with wisdom and other conquered rewards: health, a clear mind, willpower, and new perspective on life. The question that arises is what to do next. Even if they were to attempt returning to their past lives and behavior, those would no longer be satisfying in the long term, as one could only feign ignorance for so long. Alternatively, this is the moment where the now free individual chooses to return to the cave after having experienced the outside world.

Moving beyond the now finished quest can be a challenge on its own. An amusing fact that most people dismiss until they actually experience it firsthand is how breaking a fast actually requires more self-control than preparing for or even going through it. In my experience, breaking a fast properly is a thousand-fold more important than any preparation beforehand, as well as which protocol you choose to engage during it.

After going days, weeks or even months without eating solid foods, the moment you begin to chew you'll most likely want to eat much more than you should - it's as if a switch has been turned on again. Basically you're reactivating an old system of wires that relies on external stimulation.

The longer one fasted, the more important it is to break it properly. In my experience, short fasts could do with only one day, while it would be sensible to show restraint for two to three days after a week-long fast. Anyone who went for longer periods should contemplate at least a week of re-adjustment. The taste buds will be much more sensitive, which makes this a most significant opportunity to take upon new habits, relinquish the old, and appreciate the flavors of whole, unaltered foods.

Alternatively, immediately engaging in your old ways would only reinforce them, so this period is truly a double-edged sword. Don't be the hero that slayed the monster and then cut themselves with their own sword by accident...

"Every fool can fast, but only the wise knows how to break a fast properly."
-    *George Bernard Shaw*

In simple terms, one would gradually move backwards on the density levels from section 6. So a dry fast could be broken with coconut or warm water; a water fast with juices or smoothies, and a juice fast with fruits. After a few fruit meals, and seeing those being properly digested and eliminated, one could then choose to move towards salads, and eventually steamed vegetables or beyond.

It is crucial to take this process slowly in order to solidify the benefits achieved from fasting, and to avoid [at least temporarily] partaking in emotional eating at all costs. That is, don't eat what you feel like eating, but only that which you are truly hungry and salivating for. Favor small and simple meals of few ingredients and minimal to no seasoning during this period, and make it a point to chew them properly and have a peaceful environment while eating. Remember that your organs were bloated and swollen, and now have shrunk back to their original size. Aim to satisfy your hunger rather than your desires.

Through fasting, we literally change the density of our bodies by eliminating physical and emotional waste that's been lodged in there for years, and often decades. It can feel as if we now have a void inside of us [which the trash used to occupy], and we've often filled it with food out of habit. The challenge now is to learn how to accept that new density, or at least to fill these voids in a more gentle manner, such as with music, books, experiences, or at least more natural and wholesome food choices.

Remember that everything is energy [or matter] vibrating at different frequencies. So the *density* of our bodies, which is determined by what we consume on a daily basis, eventually determines the *destiny* we are aligning with. What we feel [the frequency of the electromagnetic field generated by the heart] is an indicator of which direction we're heading towards.

If one chooses to go back to their previous eating habits, it will be only a matter of time until they return to their previous state of being. Then fasting would only be a means of maintenance and expanding their lifespan, rather than a tool for self-transformation and setting a new trajectory for one's life. [Although there's nothing wrong with that!]

Alternatively, one could use this time to perform experiments and determine empirically which is best suited for themselves, rather than going by what others say. Forget diets, and see what genuinely attracts you. Anything that isn't a whole food, comes in a plastic bag or has more than 3 ingredients should be questioned though... If it is something that we would not feed babies, "sick" people or elder citizens... is it really suitable for human consumption in the first place?

Make use of your increased sensitivity and new perspective to sincerely analyse the effects of each food on your body, mind and emotional state. How you feel not only while eating, but prior to, and after. Pay attention to the whole process, from buying, to preparing, consuming and eliminating. See *how much time* you are investing (or spending) in it, and how much cleansing it requires afterwards, both in terms of your body, and of the dishes to be washed (spoiler: they are related to one another).

Did your meal leave you feeling energized, or sluggish and tired? Did it clear or fog your mind? Did it make you thirsty? Heavy and bloated, or comfortable? How long does it take for this meal to be eliminated? Does that happen before your next meal? Start counting and paying attention to your abdominal region... are things beginning to accumulate again?

Are you eating things out of addiction or necessity? You don't need to live a spartan lifestyle if you don't wish to... but it is empowering to be aware of what is the driving force behind your habits. That is, you don't have to completely quit anything you enjoy eating, but you could change the frequency or the way you eat it. It depends on the "why" you previously chose for yourself... What exactly are you aiming for?

If you have immense discipline and determination, or are facing a life-threatening condition of advanced degeneration, you could choose to go all-in, burn the bridges and never look back. Otherwise, doing a gentle transition is crucial to avoid a yo-yo effect, with periods of fasting followed by a frenzy of binge eating to re-fill the void, judging oneself, and then repeating these cycles, since you're yet to get used to the new state of being. Like a pendulum though, each time you gradually begin to keep closer and closer to the center.

Avoiding the pitfalls permanently requires sustaining permanent awareness and attention. To embrace a different lifestyle, we must allow ourselves to become a new person altogether. To embody an idealized version of ourselves, we must let go of all that's been holding us back. You can't develop new habits if you're still holding on to your old ways, just as a closed hand gripping something is not open to receiving the new.

"Dismiss whatever insults your soul."
-    *Walt Whitman*

Fasting is a tool to shift the momentum, but the change in your attitude must be permanent if you expect permanent changes in your life. Just like sitting in silent meditation is training your mind for the rest of the day, and not the end goal itself.

It is not reaching a destination or a finish line that determines who we are, but rather the walking of a specific path. The journey itself is what defines the hero. And we can only embody our truest self when we choose to create our own path, through each deliberate step that we take, rather than following someone else's. It is my intention to inspire people, not compel, so my experiences should be treated as a reference rather than an exact blueprint. Your own personal experience will always be worth more than any number of books and opinions. After all, no one knows your body better than yourself. Learn to trust it, and work together with rather than against it.

13. MY JOURNEY SO FAR

Although the first steps of my journey into health and awareness of what I'm consuming started in 2014, it was only in the second half of 2016 that I became aware of the benefits of fasting, thanks to finding John Rose's youtube channel - bless this man! At the start of 2017 I was beginning to play with my recently acquired juicer.

This book is a culmination of reading dozens of others, watching thousands of hours of youtube videos and reading many posts and stories on social media. Writing notes and reflections about my own experiences, sharing bits of my insights on youtube and facebook, playing with different ideas and protocols, talking to people who have gone through similar experiences, talking to people who have gone through different experiences, talking to people who challenge the validity of these experiences and information, observing people that follow specific diets and also experimenting with different foods myself.

Most importantly, it is the result of over four years of exploring fasting and living off less food in general, in a way that's transformed not only my health but my whole perspective of the world, the way I live and how I interact with others. It is the adoption of a lifestyle of needing less and being more.

"I fast for greater physical and mental efficiency." - Plato

For those who are interested in details, it's been four years of practicing intermittent fasting, over two years of mostly OMAD, countless 1-3 day fasts, about fifteen 7 day fasts, a handful of 10-21 day fasts, and the most important one, over 100 days of juice fasting in a row in 2020. In fact, I think I've been on liquids (sometimes smoothies or nut and seed milks) for about 200 days last year.

I write this not only as a means of self-expression, but with the intent to assist others, to dispel fears and doubts I used to have myself, and to inspire, encourage and empower whoever is in need of being so. I've kept my past self from over 5 years ago in mind, and attempted to consolidate the information that would have benefited me the most back then, but also in a way that would've reached the person I was at any point in my life.

I've got where I am now through lots of research, dedication and plenty of trial and error, so it only makes sense to attempt making this process easier for others. Humanity thrives in cooperation, not in competition.

"Employ your time in improving yourself by others writings, so that you shall come easily to what they have labored hard for."
-    *Socrates*

For example, it took me 4 attempts to make an edible green juice, and only around the 6th or 7th time did I make a combination that was truly enjoyable. Similarly, even though I was setting out for a week from start, it took me many 1-4 days fasts until I reached this primary goal, and even though there was a breakthrough around the 7th day, many months passed by until I developed the discipline to explore further.
-

Just as I thank John Rose for introducing me to juice fasting back in 2016, I am deeply grateful to Taylor Budd for presenting me the benefits of breathwork in early 2019. Ever since, I've been investing 1 to 3 hours into conscious deep breathing every day, and it's been an absolute game changer, literally enhancing all aspects of my life and bringing great clarity and insights. Starting the day with a session of breathwork or meditation sets the tone for the rest of it, and doing so at its end sets the stage for a serene and restorative night of sleep. It is a most efficient way of centering ourselves and aligning with our true nature.

Purging wise, I very often shed tears during my breathwork sessions, as well as expel mucus and gas. After a while the body begins to heat up, and on warmer days I break quite the sweat. Most of my insights and *inspiration* come during these hours.

Going beyond, I've felt that stacking those hours of consciously breathing in silence and stillness helped me become more present and comfortable in my body, and sensitive to subtle changes in its wellbeing. It becomes easier to recognize what disrupts the internal balance and the effects of each thing I consume, especially in regards to how long it takes to travel my intestines, and how much it hinders the movements of my diaphragm. I've empirically verified that a clear colon leads to a clear mind, and deep breaths lead to deep thoughts.

The next turning point was late 2019, after several months of daily breathwork and also occasionally experimenting with diatomaceous earth & herbs, I did aged orin enemas for the first time during a 21 days fast, and began passing several parasites over the following weeks. Cravings and struggles reduced drastically afterwards, and I suddenly regained a substantial degree of control over my mind and body.

From August 2019 until March 2020 I was often doing 3-7 day fasts, eating OMAD in and during early 2020, mostly raw foods. The following are a few excerpts from my journals during the 100 day juice fast I did last year, from around the March equinox to late June. It is quite amusing how the clarity of mind and the experience itself begins to fade away after you break the fast and start eating solid foods again... just like dreams are either forgotten or feel too ethereal after a while.

"It's amazing how there are still lots of solid things coming out and mad amounts of mucus everyday... The bliss of being on these high vibrations, specially at times such as these can't quite be put into words. Having a clear mind is underrated and most people have never quite experienced this. I'm sure there are even more levels beyond what I'm experiencing right now."
- *Day 34*

"Nothing tastes as good as feeling light, supple and filled with energy and vitality! The fun thing... the cleaner you get, the more you can appreciate the simple flavours of fruit; the more refined all of your senses get! I've been mostly drinking coconut water and apple juice for over a month and I still get that bit of buzz when I break the dry fasting window with either of them... so good!"
- *Somewhere in the 60s*

"Doing a solid food vacation is the most important and powerful thing any human being can do right now. It is the ultimate reclamation of your own

health, and therefore true wealth, freedom and sovereignty. Regardless of your age, health and diet, EVERYONE has way more filth stuck inside their bodies than you can possibly imagine - until you go the distance and see for yourself. [...] We've barely scratched the potential of our bodies and minds, and to cease the consumption of death and decay allows us to truly appreciate the life energy/chi/biophotons/electricity present in raw foods, in the sun and the very (clean) air we breathe. "

-      Day 75

"During my night meditation yesterday I had to get up three times in 5-7 minutes intervals or so to pass a very nasty, STICKY and muddy diarrea lol. Felt so much better afterwards, and also slept very well hah."

-      Somewhere in the 90s

"Had two very interesting and intense purges around the solstice solar eclipse weekend; on both days 93 and 96 I woke up at around 3am to head to the bathroom and I spent a good hour going back and forth... wasn't pleasant, say over 10 times and diarrhea... the first was very thick and foul smelling, second was more liquid, filled with small particles and mucus.. and a bit of a fermented smell. But I was too sleepy to properly analyse them haha. I felt low on energy during the whole weekend, where I did a few enemas and continued seeing some filth coming out.. lots of sleeping and resting. After the morning purge on the 96th I felt amazing though! I've been needing less sleep and my skin and hair have gotten smoother since."

- *Day 96*

"Woke up early and had many releases again, being not too high in energy. Already feeling much better by the evening though!"
- *Day 101*

"Waking up very early to have a release has become more common, and I'm overall seeing more movements... At the beginning of the fast it wasn't daily and I was doing 2-3 enemas per week to support it."
- *Day 104*

"Pleased by noticeable improvements in flexibility during daily yoga. No loss of strength whatsoever. BMs have been mostly mud of different degrees of thickness and mucus for a while now. Some very weird and thick mucus."
- *Day 105 (I remember I increased my time in sirsasana and sarvangasana from 3-5 minutes to up to 8 minutes each during this period!)*

"Passed two very large and robust mucus/parasite things! Been a while, seems there are still some.. about 15cm long each, and they almost had a structure to it.. and looked like there might be some eggs inside? Idk really. They had more "meat" or thickness than any other from before. [...] There can be tricky or difficult times, but man... when you hit certain shifting points... words cannot contain the excitement and joy you'll feel! Mental clarity and feeling both light and energized on all levels is PRICELESS!
- *Day 107*

Certainly not all of it were great moments, since many were the times I felt quite miserable for a few hours, or at worst a few days, until I had an adequate bowel movement to eliminate whatever it was. Though usually it was only during the minutes that preceded the event. So whenever you feel low during a fast... remember that you're in the process of eliminating something.

To balance it out, I can talk about the best moments too. There were a few glimpses of bliss and serenity that I had previously only experienced while in deep meditation, simply arising out of nowhere. Often during the dry fasting window, but also when I was drinking juice, or looking out the window, listening to music, or anything really... I would be suddenly enveloped by this overwhelming feeling of gratitude, peace and interconnectedness with all around me, which caused me to tear up and start smiling or laughing uncontrollably. It genuinely felt as if the colors got brighter and more vivid; in fact, as if all of my 5 senses were heightened even further. A sort of natural high that came from simply being in alignment with the universal rhythm.

There's a taoist saying that enlightenment feels just like everyday life, except you're about 2 inches off the ground. That is akin with the idea of being in this world, but not of this world. To care, but not carry. It seems to me that the more detached from ideas and circumstances we get, the more present we can be, and as a result, the deeper we feel and truly connect with everything and everyone around us. According to Lao Tzu, "the master is detached from all things; that is why she is one with them. Because she has let go of herself, she is perfectly fulfilled. [...] True words seem paradoxical."

I ended up breaking the fast somewhere around day 110, not because I felt I was 100% cleansed and finished, but more so on a whim. I realized I didn't feel quite ready to move further than that, as there were still a few things I wished to eat and partake in. Not to confuse with an addiction or desires though, as those almost vanished after passing all those parasites. It was simply an honest wanting of having certain experiences, at least one last time. I'd say I was simply honoring my process by breaking the fast at that point, in order to take a small detour before returning to it - although I am aware that it does sound like an excuse. Maybe it was, but I don't regret it.

Part of me also wanted to see the truth for myself, and make use of the cleansed temple to truly see the impacts different foods would have. So I set out on some experiments, coupled with 3-21 days of fasting in between (spoiler: wheat bread made me cough mucus within minutes of ingestion). At last, I've made my peace with saying goodbye to what I verified to no longer serve me.

It certainly helped that I felt absolutely miserable after eating most cooked foods, and being witness to the internal havoc they created until finally eliminated. I deeply felt how that impacted my yoga and meditative practices. Their spell remained strong though, as with each meal I'd become slightly more numb and prone to "doing it just once more". I realized I could very easily go back to where I used to be, but given my new level of awareness, it would be no different from masochism. I can clearly see the "highway to hell" and the "stairway to heaven" right in front of me, and all that distincts one from another is choice.

I also feel I understood the reason so many who push themselves into longer fasts or change their diets too quickly sometimes end up "relapsing" or changing back a few months or years later. It's good to be sure of where you want to go, and even better to have the discipline to commit to it… but it seems foolish to attempt to get there as fast as possible, rather than enjoying the journey. Moving forward with regrets is like putting a time-bomb in your closet and pretending it isn't there. I've found it most effective in the long run to exhaust my wishes and curiosity, so I'm able to leave them behind for good. We are here to have all sorts of experiences, after all. Knowing when to stop, and having the willpower to do so, you can avoid any danger.

Aside from the challenge of withstanding the emotional detox, later on, another one arises, which is a sort of boredom. The cleaner we get, the less we wish to consume. So we come to realize just how much time is wasted in buying and processing things, and we often find ourselves with a certain degree of free time (unless your occupation or family takes care of it for you).

It's interesting that both challenges can be solved in the same way: through developing any type of skill or a hobby. Wasting your time away scrolling on social media, binge watching netflix series or similar activities may have their time and place, but they should be the exception rather than the norm. We must find something productive that we enjoy, and also serves as a means of self expression - even better if it brings value to other beings, in which case you might even get paid for it.

If struck by uncertainty, I would recommend any of the following: meditation, any holistic way of moving your body, picking a musical instrument, reading books, or going for walks in nature and simply appreciating the little details, the behavior of the animals, the clouds and the stars, watching sunrises and sunsets, etc. When we're not distracted all the time, it becomes easier to realize what it is that we're really inspired to do, and actually matters to us - and what doesn't. The more we become present in the present, the more we are available to receive a present [from the Universe]. What we want is to develop ways of connecting with our intuition - then all we have to do is follow it.

Detachment has been a major theme to me in 2020. The more I fasted and cleansed my temple, the more compelled I felt to cleanse on a physical (external) level, but also mental and emotional. I was already quite adept to a minimalist lifestyle, but still found myself getting rid of more clothes, old mementos, relationships that were holding me back, beliefs that were holding me back, and all sorts of habits, belongings and other things that at some point I deemed relevant, or even essential, but not anymore. I must highlight that it was an entirely spontaneous and effortless process, and I felt much better and lighter after each "session" of cleansing.

Keep in mind that everything is temporary, with change being the only permanent aspect of life. Whether something is good or bad for us can only be determined in hindsight, as those are rather subjective concepts. That's why intuition will always be superior to logic and reason. Take the story of the chinese farmer, for example.

Once a wild horse arrived at a family's farm, and all of the neighbors gathered to say "what a fortunate thing!". The farmer replied: "maybe". Next day, his son attempted to tame the horse, fell and broke his leg. Everyone gathered to say "what an unfortunate thing!". The farmer replied: "maybe". Following day, the army came recruiting capable men to go to war, but the son was dismissed due to his injury. The neighbors gathered again to say "what a fortunate thing!". The farmer replied: "maybe". And the story goes on indefinitely, with the horse running away but then coming back with the rest of its pack, and whatever else your creativity can come up with.

So was it a good idea for me to break the fast when I was "so close" to fully cleansing my intestines, or a bad one? Who knows! I certainly don't. Maybe this book wouldn't've been written if I didn't. Maybe I would've been enlightened and left this plane of existence if I kept going. Or, maybe 5 years into the future I would end up going back to my old lifestyle and cause all sorts of disturbances and emotional confusion to myself. Maybe it will allow me to meet someone, or come across a certain piece of information, experience, insight or opportunity. Life is too unpredictable, so I find it best to simply go along with my intuition without offering any resistance.

My Way by Frank Sinatra starts playing in the background

There's no right way to detox and transform oneself... Therefore, we should each strive to do it in *our own way*. Sincerity is one of the most important things to practice.

It seems to me that most people are not really scared of starvation, as much as they are concerned with either the idea of losing muscle, or of not having their fix... which would result in facing reality and who they really are without a distraction, or a buffer in between. Many are actually afraid of realizing their true potential, as power and responsibility [ability to respond] are directly proportional to one another.

As much as the tongue and the brain may enjoy certain textures and flavors, the rest of our organs have a very different opinion. In particular, regarding the sacrifice of a clear mind and internal peace. The more often I went into fasts longer than a week, the more certain I became that chewing food is overrated. Nothing tastes as good as being healthy, light and alive feels like. Artificial (externally induced) highs will never beat natural (internally generated) highs. The latter are sustainable, long lasting, and free.

There can be no shortcuts in fasting, because we're not really walking a new path, but rather undoing a series of actions that had already been made. The only thing you can do is delay it. The path is already set, and it will be unique to each of us based on our own genetic history, upbringing, cultivated habits, and so on. Fasting is not so much about exploring new, uncharted territory, as it is about revisiting buried parts of ourselves.

Rather than achieving something, we're untangling knots and shedding away what's no longer true or necessary. The more we try to do things, the more of a mess we make. We simply have to trust and allow the body to untangle itself, by itself. The path into the light seems dark, the path forward seems to go back, and the direct path seems long.

As we venture into the depths of ourselves, fasting takes shadow work to a whole new level, which is greatly tied to the emotional detox. Through shining the light of awareness, we realize what's never been us to begin with. The greatest illusion is seeing our shadows as separate from us, or the cause of our issues, when it's the other way around. They can be temporarily suppressed, but never defeated... Because we'd only be fighting ourselves if we do so. It is much wiser to see how they can be integrated instead.

The taiji symbol gives us an accurate portrait of what it means to be a whole, integral being. It is always about balance. For instance, a spring that is too rigid and compressed would be useless, and the same applies to one that is too loose and flexible. Only when it has an ideal degree of elasticity will it be functional. With life, the key is in realizing that it's not a static or rigid balance, but rather an ongoing, fluid, wave-like flow of energies that compliment each other. It is harmony in motion: the two polarities are dancing, not fighting.

I've come to see the breath as the basis for our communication with self (spirit), as well as the bridge between the inside and the outside of our bodies. The body is a spaceship, and awareness is the pilot. Our breathing pattern is the steering wheel, and the way we feel, our metaphysical GPS. The frequency of the torus field generated by our hearts affects the structure and behavior of our cells and DNA.

Noise can be seen as scrambled, erratic, chaotic vibrations. It muffles, disturbs and disrupts efficient communication, that is, the relationship between different forms of energy. All interactions are music. The difference between music and noise is the first is harmonious with its surroundings and the universal rhythm, therefore it is self or life sustaining. Any substances we put inside of our bodies are vibrations we're processing, so most "foods", given how unnatural and modified they are, not to mention the hazardous combinations, are essentially creating noise inside of us. Ever wonder where all of those weird thoughts come from, or why it is often difficult to quiet one's mind?

The quality of the communication between our cells is the basis for our external communication with others, so the more we get rid of the mucus and the filth that is in the way, the less we perceive separation, which is essentially an illusion that comes from impaired or inefficient communication.

When two people are arguing and failing to understand each other, they're often shouting. When two lovers communicate, they do so in whispers, if not inaudibly, through their eyes, facial expressions and subtle body movements. When there is no artificial distance or obstructions present, that is, when the hearts are in tune with one another, it can be perceived that everything is contained in silence.

"To need nothing is divine, and the less a man needs the nearer does he approach to divinity." - Socrates

I would like to suggest the reader to forget about "calories", and think in terms of electricity instead. If this sounds weird, how about comparing how you feel after consuming stale or cooked foods versus drinking fresh fruit or vegetable juice? There's a certain electricity, or aliveness, in the latter... Some people call it biophotons, where bio stands for life, and photons for light. Check kirlian photography. From my perspective, it is akin to what other cultures refer to as prana, qi, vital force, etc. Its presence is what separates organic (living) matter from inorganic (dead). Certain foods have more or less of it, depending on how they were cultivated and prepared, but there are many different sources of and ways of absorbing it.

Before I used the example of how cars work on liquid fuel, but in truth, nowadays they, and many other machines, work on electricity, or directly harness energy from the sun, just like trees and vegetation. So what's stopping us from doing the same? Perhaps we already are, and just haven't fully acknowledged it, or have been doing it inefficiently.

It is said that about 98% of our DNA is "junk", and that we only utilize a fraction of our brain's capacity. This just means that science hasn't matured enough to understand our own potential, which as far as I'm concerned, might as well be limitless. The question is, are we evolving, or are we devolving? From the dictionary, devolving means "to pass on or delegate to another", while evolving, "to develop or achieve gradually". So the more reliant we become on external gadgets and drugs, the more we devolve... While developing and integrating our mind, body and spirit, and harnessing our skills, is true evolution.

If the technology is getting smarter... maybe people are getting dumber. It is worth pondering at which point we stop using technology, and technology begins to use us. What we need is to develop organic, sustainable technology that supports our needs without disrupting the harmony of nature and of our own bodies.

The artificial path is pointing to humans becoming cyborgs by merging with the machines [and we're halfway there with our reliance on smartphones and computers, by the way]. Maybe the organic path, of reconnecting with living nature, will allow us to unlock more of our body and DNA's potential and become actual magicians or x-humans. I can't predict the future, but I'd rather engage in pleasant dreams than in nightmares.

Being fasted is our natural state of being, while drinking and eating are voluntary acts. Whether those are actually necessary or not to sustain our bodies will be left for a future book, after I further cleanse this vessel and explore the realms of dry fasting. But at the very least, through allowing oneself to fast for longer periods of time, it can be acknowledged that we need way less than we're taught. Reducing our needs is the fastest road to true sovereignty.

There's no such thing as high or low energy, only stable or unstable, coherent or chaotic. When there are no obstructions, energy can flow without attrition. The less attrition there is, the more self-sustaining the system becomes. Many things are only considered to be i'm-possible because no one's dared to prove them otherwise.

Nothing fancy is required in order for us to manifest our true potential. Each of us is either the hero we've always waited for, or the villain that ruins our lives. It is our choice to decide which role we're more inclined to play and embody. The grass is not greener on the other side; the grass is greener where we water it. Infinite possibilities, power and all of the answers we seek are waiting for us within ourselves - all we have to do is claim them.

The first step is becoming aware of it, but knowledge by itself is static. For it to be useful, it must be either applied or shared with others: wisdom is knowledge put in motion. There's a reason I keep talking about self-mastery or discipline... without it, even if we know what we must do, we won't be able to take charge of our lives and align with our dreams and inspiration. We can only fail if we fail to convince ourselves.

"Be ye doers of the word, and not hearers only, deceiving your own selves." -   James 1:22

The real treasure is within. Like sculpting a statue of a greek God or Goddess, we don't have to add anything to the marble... we simply remove all of the impurities and the superfluous matter until they are revealed, in all their glory and beauty.

"Fasting cures disease, dries up bodily humors, puts

demons to flight, gets rid of impure thoughts, makes the mind clearer and the heart purer, the body sanctified, and raises man to the throne of God."

- *Athenaeus*

What if we're all [God], playing all of the different parts in this ongoing show? Just as we have days and nights, summers and winters, we also have the seasons of the great year in accordance to the precession of the equinoxes (25920 earthly years). Easy parallels can be made: during the day we are awake, during the night we are asleep. During summer all of the trees and plants are thriving and the animals are out and about. During winter, plenty of vegetation dies, and many animals hibernate. One period is bright, with plenty of energy flowing, while the other is dark and a time for resting and replenishing.

The same goes for life in general: everything is fractal. Perhaps we're all miniature Trees of Life, with our spine being the rainbow bridge, and the chakras, the different worlds. During the Iron Age (winter), most of [God] is asleep, as dormant seeds. During the Golden Age (summer), most of it is awake, as blossoming flowers and trees. Right now, most of us are asleep, very few are awake, and many are in the process of waking up, as we are moving into the age of aquarius.

For instance, the Bible (script-ur-e) makes a lot more sense to me by replacing "holy spirit" for whole breaths, "bread" for breath, "man" or "husband" for mind, "woman" or "wife" for body, "christ" for awareness and "God" for I AM. Not to mention that it seems to be all about symbolism rather than factual history.

From that perspective, each and all of us would be [potentially] Jesus: the savior or the hero of the story. To wait for him or another messiah to be born elsewhere would be a sort of self-denial. It is referred to as a virgin birth because it's an awareness or identity born from within us. Mary, the mother, being a *pure* body, gives birth to "Christ Consciousness" or awareness, without assistance from Joseph, the mind or the ego, but depending only on the Holy Spirit, that is, the universal breath of life.

This awareness is like a seed that has been buried within all of us, and sprouts only when the necessary conditions are met, which will vary for each individual.

We'll also find plenty of references to similar processes of internal alchemy in other cultures, all centered in the idea of the purification of our vessel, followed by the integration of body, mind and spirit that ultimately gives birth to a light, diamond or rainbow body that is capable of transcending this three-dimensional realm. Mer-ka-ba (a star tetrahedron, which represents the integration of the two polarities) literally means light-spirit-body, but further exploring these themes, sacred geometry, vortex math and esoteric practices would be derailing from this book's initial purpose. Maybe next time.

Dreaming (living as a human) is like a game of hide and seek with [God]. For it to take place, we must first forget our identity, or where we have hidden, otherwise it would be no fun. After going through all sorts of experiences, we begin to wake up when we eventually get tired of playing. We mature and remember who we are, just as an acorn grows into an oak tree, which in turn produces more acorns. Human is [God] asleep, represented in the movie by Neo. [God] is human awake, represented by the One. Only personal choices separate the two states of being. They are one and the same, as we are *all-one in cycles of consciousness*.

Apocalypse means disclosure, or unveiling. Maybe there is going to be a cataclysmic event that will change the world, but I'm more inclined to believe this is rather an internal process. As we change our perception of ourselves, the world around us and the way we experience it change accordingly. In that sense, the end of the world won't happen to us - it will happen through us, as we become aware of our true nature. We are the apocalypse, and it is as much of an ending as it is a new beginning.

"You are here for no other purpose than to realize your inner divinity and manifest your innate enlighten-

ment." -   *Morihei Ueshiba*

Trauma, whether physical or psychological, causes cells to be suffocated. The damage disrupts the fractality of our template and the connection between our cells, isolating an area of the body [and/or of the mind]. This results in us forgetting part of who we are, which is akin to falling asleep, creating an illusion of being separated from whatever that suppressed part represents. To heal, or to become whole again, is a process of reintegrating all of these severed areas and cells of our body, fully inhabiting it, and waking up to who we truly are.

We eat to forget. Then we fast to remember.

Thank you for reading.

Luccas Laq
February, 2021.

Any and all sincere feedback is appreciated, so please share your reviews if you feel inclined to do so.

I also have ideas for 4 other titles, which have all been foreshadowed here. So depending on how this book is received, stay tuned for more. Remember to never take my words more seriously than your own experience though.

For the time being, I can also be found on facebook, gab or telegram under the same name. To anyone who is able and feels inclined to support, I would welcome any contribution via paypal to luccaslaq@protonmail.com.

"I can only show you the door. You're the one who has to walk through it."
  -     *Morpheus*

Printed in Great Britain
by Amazon